BREAKING THE INTERNET

HOW ONE COMMUNITY IS WORKING TOWARD DIGITAL EQUITY

Terrence Denoyer

Foreword by
Lauren Tavarez

Wells Smith Books

Mystic, Connecticut
WellsSmithBooks.com

© 2021 by Terrence Denoyer

Editor: Amanda Smith
Copy Editor: Frank Ferreri
Proofreaders: David Irwin, Kellie Wilks
Cover: Damonza.com
Interior: Createbook.org

First printing November 2021.

Library of Congress Cataloging-in-Publication Data
Names: Denoyer, Terrence - author
Title: Breaking the Internet | How One Community is Working
Toward Digital Equity
Description: Mystic, CT : Wells Smith Books, LLC (2021)

ISBN 978-0-578-94192-9
ISBN 978-0-578-94193-6 (ebook)

*For families everywhere who cannot get or afford
high-speed broadband in their homes.*

CONTENTS

FOREWORD

WE ALL HAVE MOMENTS in life... moments that make us stop. Literally stop everything. Stop breathing, stop moving, what feels like we stop being able to think. I was reminded of a "stop moment" when I connected with Terry to reflect on my experiences this last year navigating the COVID-19 pandemic as the Director of Digital Learning and a team member of Ector County Independent School District in Odessa, Texas.

This particular "stop moment" happened for me in mid-April of 2020; our school doors had been closed and the news had just been shared that students and staff wouldn't be returning to our campuses that spring. For a month or so prior, the news of the pandemic had been creeping closer and closer to our lives, our families, our students, and our city — and the uncertainty of what we were facing seemed overwhelming at times. Our district team had been running on adrenaline for several weeks.

This "stop moment" occurred as I collaborated with the team tasked in designing what learning would look like for our students participating from their homes. A cross section of experts and rock stars in our district came together to imagine and enhance the remote learning and teaching experience. Folks from various departments worked inspiringly as one team with a "let's go" attitude, as it felt in some ways like the rest of the world was coming to a stop. Ector County ISD had distributed over 30,000 learning devices to our students and a new digital learning framework had been created; our next step was to design lesson plans for teachers that could be used in the upcoming weeks.

As we brainstormed together, we got on a roll — resources, strategies, and activity possibilities were flying. I was thrilled to be a part of this conversation and to see so many sharing #edtech tools and ways to incorporate them into learning for our kids. This celebration was stopped short when a thought came to mind — the thought that caused the "stop moment" — what about our students without the internet? Would we be able to provide them the same experience without all of these great technology tools? The air left the room (or the virtual conference), as we came upon the realization that the lack of access to the internet many of our students faced was not something we would be able to immediately correct. There was no lesson plan available for that.

At the onset of the pandemic, Ector County ISD was able to provide devices for students, professional learning for teachers, and a variety of resources guiding parents. What we could not provide many of our students was a reliable connection to the internet at home. Throughout this experience, there has been much cause for heartbreak but none greater than our being unable to reach students because of where they live or what their family budget might afford, at no fault of their own. These students without an internet connection have been unable to join their classes online during a time they needed these connections the most. The long-term effects of this has yet to be seen but the predictions for these students are devastating.

The internet is not an abstract cloud. It is constructed

of cables, conduit, electricity, glass, light (optics), data centers with servers and racks, protocols, and many other things. It can be constructed poorly. And, it can be broken. I still remember when the selfie taken by Bradley Cooper at the Oscars with Ellen DeGeneres' phone got retweeted so much in a short span of time, it took Twitter down for about 20 minutes. The phrase that something viral had broken the internet started trending in itself, but this is not just a figure of speech. The signals coming from hundreds of thousands of phones and computers travelling over the infrastructure of the internet simultaneously overloaded Twitter's data center capacity, causing it to shut down like Texas in a cold snap.

If the internet can be broken, then it can be designed — and made better. It can be engineered and constructed to reach more people at high speeds. That is the premise of this book.

When I was asked to compose this foreword, to say I was thrilled is an understatement. I say with great pride that the future of this situation is in excellent hands following the lead of Ector County ISD and our many supporters. I applaud the leadership and unwavering commitment to do what is right, modeled by Dr. Scott Muri and Dr. Kellie Wilks and the connection to a larger stage for this conversation from author Terry Denoyer. All students, in Ector County ISD and beyond, have a right to learn and pursue their potential; this work is not done until all children and their families have that capability. It is for this reason these conversations must continue until we break down the inequalities of the internet and deliver digital equity.

Lauren Tavarez

Two students — two different experiences.

One learner lives in the neighborhood where gigabit internet service is wired directly into her home. Leena has dreams of going to Stanford and majoring in computer science. She is taking several coding courses, even in seventh grade; one through school and one online through Outschool in the evenings. Leena regularly works with data and code sets, pulling down and uploading to Github and Hadoop on a near daily basis. Her side hustle is as a YouTube sensation — or rather her bulldog, Bugsy, has his own channel full of content that Leena films, edits, and uploads a few times a week. Her internet connection never flinches, and she almost never even has to think about it.

The other learner lives in a part of town where the only internet option is DSL, provided by the phone company. Julia loves reading about biology and wants to be a zoologist one day. Julia and her family of four share the home internet connection, and there is rarely a moment when someone in the house isn't using the Wi-Fi for something. She tries to attend class online but often drops off her Zoom call. She completes some assignments online but isn't always able to access the videos and interactive content her teacher sends out. She starts to fall behind in math, and though there is an online tutoring service offered by her school, her connection isn't fast enough to connect to it. With the constant drops, buffering, and slowness, Julia gets frustrated doing anything on a laptop.

Author's Note

THIS IS A STORY ABOUT striving for digital equity.

To put it mildly, economic and educational opportunities are increasingly accessed via the internet. Many understood this previously, but the COVID-19 pandemic magnified it. As a result, homes and businesses need to be connected to the internet. Those that aren't constitute the "digital divide." Communities of color, Tribal lands, and rural communities are disproportionately impacted by this divide. So, if a large portion of our population cannot get high-speed home internet because they cannot afford it, or there is none where they live, then something is broken. Or, more accurately, something needs to be broken.

"Digital Equity is a condition in which all individuals and communities have the information technology capacity needed for full participation in our society, democracy and economy. Digital Equity is necessary for civic and cultural participation, employment, lifelong learning, and access to essential services," according to the National Digital Inclusion Alliance (NDIA).[1]

As a society, we need a broader range of people to participate in discussions of what their communities and businesses need from the telecommunications industry. There is a tendency to exclude "laypeople" from conversations about broadband, (and technology, generally, for that matter). A lack of agency or general reluctance to engage might perpetuate because people do not see themselves as "technology people." Some might not feel adequately informed of the ever-fluxing and historically complicated telecommunications and information services industries. They might face conversations with "technology people" steeped in obfuscation and the power dynamics of jargon. Or they might understand quite a lot about community internet access and yet feel powerless against the centralization of oligopolistic, "big tech" forces. This book is an attempt to crack the wall that is the barrier to the transparency needed by local community leaders facing connectivity challenges.

When more people are involved in discussions (and planning) of community broadband, more ideas are brought to the table. Marginalized groups can contribute new perspectives and new insights. When the goal becomes one of connecting everyone, a more diverse chorus of voices is needed to contribute their needs and question assumptions. It is not just the right thing to do. From a logistical standpoint, this results in a more realistic and feasible plan and therefore, one more likely to succeed. From a community standpoint, the benefits of planning holistically are well documented — more broadband connectivity leads to a more educated people, more jobs, more health options, and more business.

In researching the history of home broadband, I came upon this problem: That millions of people in the U.S. (billions, globally) do not have high-speed internet broadband in their home. This problem was not new. I didn't discover it. But I wanted to help. And as I began learning more, I found surprisingly few books that could inform the strategies of an underserved community looking to solve the problem, explaining to them their options plainly, or at minimum, highlighting proactive strategies other communities have pursued. A few organizations do this incredibly well, and their research can be accessed on the web, including the Benton Foundation, the Institute for Local Self-Reliance (ILSR), and *Broadband Communities* magazine. There are others too. They highlight critically important concepts and dive deep into case studies of people around the country taking the issue into their own hands at the local level. I find the ILSR and Community Broadband Networks' podcasts (*Broadcast Bits* and *Connect This!*) to be highly entertaining and informative. I can't thank these folks enough for my own individual education on the topic. But still, when learning, I personally just love to sink into a book. So, I thought, "Maybe that's something I could offer."

In the following chapters, I have intentionally tried to minimize techno-speak and industry jargon to invite a broader range of folks to the table. This book is for the mayor or city council member of the small town where internet service just isn't offered and voters are clamoring for solutions. It is for the chamber of commerce or economic development board member who is looking to stimulate growth and attract businesses to their region. It is for the community leaders who are looking to solve the problem of home internet access for families in their neighborhoods. Similarly, it is for city planners and technology managers designing or upgrading their infrastructure. It is for the staff and leaders of utility cooperatives and local ISPs expanding their service, looking for a customer-centric view of the planning process. This book is for these folks to envision something more equitable for their communities in all senses of the word.

This is a story about envisioning various options or pathways down which the community can travel to solve their broadband problem(s), and so, types of network technology will be discussed intermittently in the book. Here is a quick and dirty glossary of home internet access terms you will encounter. (Don't worry — it's only a page or so.)

- **5G** refers to the technical standard for the next generation – the fifth generation – of mobile connectivity. (Due to projected high speeds, many have been wondering if it can serve the needs of a family in a home.)

- **Bandwidth** is the maximum rate of data transfer across a given path. (Wikipedia)

- **Broadband** refers to high-speed internet access. (The term arose in the effort to distinguish from the category of dial-up services but has since come to denote *high-speed*.)

- **Cable internet service** sends data over existing co-axial wires originally installed for cable television.

- **Dark fiber** is fiber optics infrastructure not currently in use but planned for a future deployment.

- **Digital inclusion** refers to a series of programs and efforts to grow digital literacy and connect those that need it with internet service.

- **Digital subscriber line (DSL) service** sends data over existing copper wires originally installed for telephone service.

- **Electromagnetic (EM) spectrum** is composed of radio waves and other forms of energy (radiation), required for wireless communications.

- **Fiber optics** send data via light through thin glass fibers; it is generally acknowledged as the highest capacity type of fixed connection.

- **Fixed** describes an internet service that supplies connectivity to a building like a home or business, as opposed to a mobile or cellular service.

- **Fixed wireless service** provides internet to homes wirelessly using radio links between stationary sites, (with one side connected to fiber optics).

- **Gbps** (Gigabits per second) is a measure of speed for data traveling over a network (equivalent to 1,000 Mbps).

- **Internet service provider (ISP)** is a company or other entity offering internet service to consumers; this book primarily discusses those that deliver service to a resident's home.

- **Last Mile networks** represent the local connection between the home or wireless subscriber and the ISP.

- **Mbps** (Megabits per second) a measure of speed for data traveling over a network, often reported as download and upload speed (e.g. 25Mbps/3Mbps)

- **Mesh Wi-Fi** refers to a method of Wi-Fi deployment utilizing multiple transmitters that repeat a Wi-Fi signal and spread the reach of the network.

- **Middle Mile Networks** connect data locally (on the "last mile") to an internet backbone. Sometimes referred to as "backhaul."

- **Telco** a telecommunications company that provides internet service.

PREFACE

AS THE PANDEMIC SHUTDOWN loomed in late winter of 2020, Superintendent Dr. Scott Muri, Ed.D. realized that COVID-19 had just moved the goalposts on an existing problem. A problem he knew all too well.

Having fought for digital inclusion much of his career, the pandemic represented a new villain in the saga. Dr. Muri sat at his desk in the mostly empty district office in Odessa, Texas. The sky outside was gloomy and overcast. Students and staff were about to head off on Spring Break, and Scott would soon get a phone call informing him that his schools would be closed much longer than that. The community's response to the pandemic would require thoughtful planning. He remembered back to his days of teaching, when he first saw the potential of technology to help kids learn outside the walls of the classroom, and also the first time he witnessed how inequities in the system could leave kids behind.

Despite his height (he's tall), Scott's leadership style and character are not overbearing or intimidating. His disposition is warm and friendly, and his approach is always collaborative. Residents in the community are often thanking him profusely for the great work he is doing for their kids. But what keeps him up at night are the obstacles to learning his students are facing at any given point in time. "I was lucky to discover early in life that serving children was my purpose and became dedicated to providing high-quality academic experiences to prepare children for success. I look at my purpose as my "why," and it drives all of my leadership decisions," Scott would later write. "My job is to facilitate all of the pieces, from administration to the classroom, that enable our teachers to have great learning experiences with their students. However, in my 33 years as an educator, I had never before experienced anything like this."[1]

Scott believes in *personalization*. It means meeting every student where they are — not giving everyone the same thing as a default. It hasn't always been called that, and what Scott has learned well over the course of his career is that it isn't one thing. Technology is a piece of it, but so is developing teachers, among other things. But to bring all those pieces together in the midst of a global pandemic, students and teachers had to have adequate connectivity in the home.

Dr. Scott Muri has worn a lot of hats in K-12 education. He is a National Board Certified Teacher and taught for eight years in Newland, North Carolina, in the 1990s. He was then a dean of students, assistant principal, and principal of a high school in Florida. Charlotte-Mecklenburg Schools (CMS) hired him in 2007 as an area superintendent, later promoted him to a zone superintendent, and then he briefly took on the role of chief information officer for the district.

Scott worked for CMS for five years before being offered the role of deputy superintendent of academics at Fulton County Schools (FCS) in Atlanta. He and his team at FCS worked tirelessly to develop a personalized learning framework for the district's 96,000 students. In 2015, he accepted the position of superintendent of schools of Spring Branch Independent School District (SBISD) in the Houston area, and in 2019, he was offered the job of superintendent of Ector County Independent School District (ECISD), also in Texas.

Upon arriving to Odessa, Scott began hearing anecdotes of families' issues with home internet connectivity in the region. Many non-profit coalition and advocacy groups, like the Permian Strategic Partnership, had zeroed in on the issue before the pandemic, and Scott discussed the issue with them, thinking it might be something they could work on together. He became focused on learning more about the problem. "We knew as a school system that we had families that didn't have high-speed internet access in their home. We weren't quite sure how many, but we knew we had some families that did not have that opportunity," Scott would later state to the Odessa City Council, "Therefore, we knew that some of our kids would not be able to learn and engage with their teachers. We also knew that some of our own teachers didn't have internet access in their home. So they were going to have trouble engaging with their students and the work. But we weren't quite sure how big the problem was."

Scott was aware that, nationally, progress had been made in expanding broadband access in recent years. The telecommunications industry estimated it made capital investments of $795 billion in fixed broadband infrastructure from 2009 through 2017, according to a report by the U.S. Government Accountability Office (GAO). These investments have made a big difference for a lot of U.S. households in the past decade. The GAO report states "that fixed broadband service was available to 94.4% of the U.S. population in 2018, up from 81.2% in 2012, although affordability and digital literacy remain barriers to adoption and use. While service availability for people in rural areas increased from 45.7% in 2012 to 77.7% in 2018, service in rural areas continues to lag behind urban areas, according to FCC's broadband availability report."[2] We will delve into the accuracy of this data and the adequacy of the government's definition of "broadband" in Chapter 2. It was well understood that despite noble efforts and progress, there were still many households without high-speed internet.

Before the pandemic, there were fragmented efforts to address the equity problem. Digital equity, or digital inclusion, in education is the condition of *all* students having access to the right tools (e.g. a laptop, tablet) plus a reliable internet connection. Nationwide and locally, efforts had been planned, executed, and spotlighted. Laptop "1:1" programs and mobile hotspots had been deployed in many school districts and communities (Ector County included). Philanthropists and states had donated funding — but the problem remained. Some called it the "homework" gap.

Then, all schoolwork became *home*work. And for the students who didn't have home internet access when their schools closed in 2020, school just... stopped.

Picture it. Nearly springtime in west Texas. In the interest of public health, schools closed and students were instructed to stay home—but schoolwork still an expectation. The internet as the solution. Most were capable of doing *some* schoolwork remotely, in theory, interacting with their teachers on Zoom, Meet, or

Teams, submitting their assignments, etc.—but many simply without the connectivity in their home to do so. Or perhaps, they had low-performance connectivity in their homes, which tended to freeze or just drop them entirely. Confusion and frustration ensued. The traditional learning process for many kids simply stopped.

Scott and the staff at Ector County Independent School District (ECISD) worked diligently in the initial days of the pandemic to launch their online learning materials, including coordinating and distributing paper-based assignments and materials. That there were gaps in home internet connectivity around Ector County was well-known by members of the community—just not to what scale. To mitigate, thousands of copies of the paper-based assignments were printed in the spring of 2020. Scott describes the coordination setup with "literally, cafeterias *full*. With sorting areas for teachers."

Scott and ECISD also partnered with several local cable television stations to film and broadcast helpful tips and educational content to families on TV as the pandemic kept everyone home. Local PBS, Telemundo, and CW affiliates provided time, and ECISD provided the content, with Scott hosting the hour-long program, leaning on the volunteerism of his teachers to provide lessons and other guidance.

"We went after television, because we knew the internet wasn't an option for a lot of our families," Scott explained, "And it wasn't going to happen right away, so we thought, *how can we get something to them quickly?*" Scott hoped these alternative formats would be helpful to those that needed them and mitigate the gaps in internet service, at least somewhat. At a time when the rest of the world was increasing their reliance on digital technologies at a scale never before seen, Scott and his team also had to travel back in time to meet the needs of those disconnected. The time commitment to filming and producing the content ultimately proved too much for Scott and his teachers, and they would eventually phase this out. Yet, the paper-based materials and TV content were utilized by thousands of households at the onset of and throughout the pandemic in 2020.

But still, Scott did not see these formats as a substitution for the real thing. From day one of the pandemic shutdown in the spring of 2020, many students were simply not able to learn and interact with their teachers and peers the ways they were accustomed to, setting back their academic progress, possibly for life. Scott and others predicted a "COVID slide," or regression of student progress, when school would resume in the fall.

ECISD teachers did whatever it took to intervene for the good of their disconnected students at the onset and throughout the COVID-19 pandemic, (usually phone calls). But chasing down parents is resource-intensive and yet another thing on the plate of teachers. Teachers' plates increasingly resembled something more like buffet-size serving platters.

The world decided to address the pandemic from a business standpoint by simply working from home and interacting on Zoom. Most believe this is not optimal compared to the in-person experience, but there seemed no other choice when staring down a global pandemic and following the science of social distancing. A lot has been and will continue to be discussed about whether this was a good thing or a bad thing from a productivity standpoint. This book does not debate that in-person classroom learning, under most conditions, is best for kids. This book is about taking action for those students who couldn't *just go on Zoom*. When the rest of the world is effectively able to carry on, but these kids cannot — that is a problem.

Scott Muri labeled it a crisis and sprang into action.

Chapter 1
UNDERSTAND THE PROBLEM

All that child wants is a chance. And our job is to give every one of them chances to succeed. And they will make all of us proud.
— Congressman James Clyburn (D-SC)[1]

I'm optimistic. The pandemic unmasked this whole issue and folks now, they don't roll their eyes anymore when you talk about broadband.
— Congressman Charles "Doc" Anderson (R-TX)[2]

One morning, years before the pandemic, a principal in Odessa arriving early to school that morning, as principals do, parked her car and was walking into the building. Out of the corner of her eye, she noticed an unusual sight. Not far from the building, lying on one the playground picnic tables was a student, sleeping. She approached and woke him.

"Why are you here?" she inquired. It was about 6:30 a.m.

The student groggily opened his eyes and took in his surroundings for a moment. He looked up at her.

"Well," he sighed, "I don't have Wi-Fi at home and I needed to finish my homework... and I guess I just fell asleep."

This story is not unique to Ector County. What follows on these pages is a similar story as those playing out in the southwestern United States, southeast, west, north, and east. In big cities, small towns, and Tribal lands. Globally, even. What follows is not a story *about* Texas *per se*. It is simply set in Texas. Odessa is home to Permian High School (among other schools), the setting of *Friday Night Lights,* a book, movie, and TV show of the same name. Odessa and its surrounding rural communities and small towns make up the 900 square miles that is Ector County in western Texas, not far from New Mexico's southeast border.

The region experienced significant growth in the past decade, with Ector County's population growing from about 137,000 in 2010 to about 166,000 in 2019. The landscape is literally dotted with oil rigs like many of its neighboring counties. If you view the satellite imagery from above in Google Earth, you can see the oil industry's fingerprints in thousands of little, pale dots across the region. In "booms" and "busts," production of oil generates a lot of jobs and wealth in west Texas.

Broadband is a problem throughout the state of Texas. In studying the progress of broadband development in unserved areas, the Governor's Broadband Development Council found that "over 300,000 locations in Texas are unserved. As of July 2020, an estimated 926,859 Texans do not have access to broadband at home."[3] Scott was hearing from his families and his teachers that this was a problem in Ector County. People were isolated due to the pandemic, and that isolation was compounded by a lack of connectivity. It was a barrier to learning. A barrier to commerce. A barrier to healthcare. The cruelest part of the virus may have been its proficiency at isolation and disconnection.

Jessica Rosenworcel and John B. King Jr., writing for *Education Week* as schools were about to re-open in the fall of 2020, outlined the dilemma, "More than 70% of educators assign homework that requires the internet. As a result, before the pandemic, these students without Wi-Fi access at home resorted to seeking out venues that offered it for free. They were the students nursing a drink at a fast-food restaurant, or sitting on the library steps with a laptop while they typed out their papers, or lingering in the school parking lot to complete their homework long after the final bell rang. But now the homework gap has turned into a devastating learning chasm with so many students disconnected during this pandemic at the same time as schooling moved online this spring."[4]

Scott and ECISD committed to getting every student in the district a device, such as a laptop or a tablet. It was articulated and executed in the district's strategic plan and in bulk purchases that would be made for 37,000 devices in the spring of 2020. Devices were distributed to ECISD schools who then used their libraries' inventory and distribution processes to allow students to "check out" a personal student device, just like a book — but keep it, indefinitely. A drive-thru type of system was even devised for when schools were closed.

For that technology to be effective at home, they had to connect at home. Scott quickly determined that he needed better visibility into the extent and roots of the home internet problem in Ector County, what others nationally had done to address it, and what Ector County's options were to address the problem.

Within the city limits of Odessa there are multiple

options for home internet service, like cable, DSL, and even fiber optic service in some places. Names like AT&T, Grande, and Sparklight cover much of the town. But outside the city limits of Odessa, there are far fewer internet service providers and options. And those that are there tend to be smaller, less well-known companies that tend not to invest a lot in marketing. The average consumer might not even know they are there. These providers most often deliver the internet through satellite or fixed wireless services. Satellite internet service has been around for some time, and while these services are evolving, they have not been generally regarded as high-speed, historically.

And what does "high-speed" even mean today? Does it mean the same thing to everyone? No native of the telecom industry and relatively new to Ector County, Scott set out to collaborate with others in the community whose constituencies were similarly affected by the pandemic. A natural teammate and collaborator but also a pragmatist, Scott believes firmly that any solution "takes a village." Already a member of several city council committees and state task forces, he began reaching out to local government and business leaders. He made a lot of phone (and Zoom) calls. He attended local and national meetings where he found other community leaders facing similar challenges with the pandemic and shutdown. He reached out to local business and government leaders. He reached out to philanthropies, colleges and universities, business coalitions, and other organizations active in the community. Many grasped the problem before Scott even said a word.

The pandemic had shone a light on the necessity of internet access for people of all ages and locales.

Students. Remote workers. Local businesses. Anyone that might need a doctor. Scott found peers and partners desperate to identify a solution. They discussed the urgency and scale of the problem. "Remote work has made even the affluent realize this is important," one community leader in Ector County said. Ector County Public Library saw a marked increase in the usage of its computer lab and public Wi-Fi as many adults were left without work as everything shut down. Scott could sense that the time for a collective plan of action for his county, and possibly the region, was now.

But rather than just dialing up vendors (no pun intended) looking for networking products, Scott felt he needed to better understand the problem. He wanted to conduct an objective scan of the landscape that would help build awareness among the decision-makers. A collaborative effort to discuss potential solutions could carve out space to discuss ideas (namely, a task force), pull in expert feedback, and identify the best delivery model for Ector County. A quantifiable analysis of those options (scenarios) could inform the decision, and then a roadmap to get there could show the way.

In parallel, Scott and his team worked directly with several local internet service providers in the initial days of the pandemic. He found two of the big cable companies in the region, Grande and Sparklight, willing to take action to connect families on an emergency basis (where they already provided service), and even negotiated lower rates and suspended reconnection fees to ease the burden during the shutdown. He found a donor who was willing to subsidize the subscription fees for families of low-income for twelve months. It was a big, if quiet, win. Unfortunately, Grande and Sparklight's coverage areas were primarily within the city limits of Odessa and not much of the surrounding towns in the county, leaving those outside the city limits with little or no high-speed options.

Scott was well aware there were other short-term solutions available, like providing Wi-Fi access in school parking lots or distributing hotspots to families in need (and ECISD leveraged these, as well). Some call these "band-aid" solutions because they are not without drawbacks and they are not sustainable solutions. Scott thought, *do we plan as if this is a one-time event, or do we learn from this crisis and work to ensure everyone is connected to home internet services in the future?* And so, he began working towards a longer-term, scalable strategy for the community. Even if there was never another pandemic shutdown, he believed strongly that learning didn't happen just inside the walls of a classroom. The homework gap was real, and closing it would be a huge win for his students and community.

Scott told me, "We have families that will simply accept whatever is provided by the commercial ISP market. And right now, with city and other community leaders, we can push on the industry a bit to get better options for our families.

"I don't want to own the solution. That is not my goal. But there are families with really bad options, and that just isn't right. If not us, then who is going to step up for our families?"

Despite emerging and innovative services, Scott did not think he would wake up one day and everyone in the community would be magically connected to high-speed internet. Without someone stepping up, the inequities would simply persist. And the gaps in the digital divide would widen amidst a pandemic disproportionately impacting communities of color and those economically disadvantaged.

How long the effort might take, or what the solution even was, was not yet known, of course. To figure that out was the goal. To begin coordinating this initiative with its unclear horizon, Scott leaned on his chief technology officer at ECISD, Kellie Wilks, Ed.D., who was overseeing the completion of the district's new network installation project at the time, connecting all elementary, middle, and high schools in the county with a new fiber optic service. Dr. Wilks, a veteran of the ECISD leadership team and a long-time resident of the area, knew enough about her community to understand there was an access problem even before looking at the data on the subject.

Kellie was a fifth-grade teacher early in her career and believed in the power of computers to help spark kids' interest and learning beyond the classroom walls. Her students were makers (before that was a term), learning everything from photo editing to TV and FM broadcasting. She remembers even back to the early 2000s how many of her students wanted to do even more with content production but were constrained by having to use the equipment at school. And then, she observed firsthand as personal devices and the internet steadily changed all of that.

Kellie remembers how it started slowly with the posting of high school schedules online, moving to Google Classroom in the 2010s. Then, the pandemic just exponentially accelerated everyone's experience with, and awareness of, digital learning. And Scott and Kellie realized that to take sustainable, long-term measures, they needed accurate data on who was and wasn't connected in the community. *What specific neighborhoods in Ector County lacked high speed options? How many families couldn't afford what was available? Did families want better options? How have other communities solved this problem?*

Kellie and Scott reached out to David Irwin, a co-founder of the education consulting firm, Thru (also co-founded by your distinguished author), to help with the research and to advise on options. Our team's experience working with school districts and local government agencies to help solve similar problems positioned us to tackle the challenge. We are great with research and data, and we connect dots. Our team is not comprised of telecommunications industry veterans. We were outsiders in that respect. We had worked with Scott in his former positions at Spring Branch ISD and Fulton County Schools. More than any solution (or vendor) or even feasibility study, what he wanted to do first was to accurately frame the problem and build community consensus on a long-term plan. And he needed a small team to help him navigate the ocean of stakeholder agendas, policy, and data.

And so, the initial planning team was formed.

Chapter 2

MIND THE GAP

There are 12 million students in this country who fall into the homework gap and lack the regular broad-band access they need to just do nightly schoolwork. From my perspective, this is the cruelest part of the digital divide, and it's a divide we're going to have to address, and a gap we're going to have to fix.
— Jessica Rosenworcel, Acting Chairwoman of the FCC (then Commissioner)[1]

When we invest in broadband infrastructure, we invest in opportunity for all Americans. In 2021, we should be able to bring high-speed internet to every family in America — regardless of their zip code.
— Senator Amy Klobuchar (D-MN)[2]

AMONG ITS 166,223 RESIDENTS, Ector County has about 34,000 students attending 43 ECISD schools and centers. There are 52,530 households in the county, and the population of Odessa proper is just over 120,000 people at the time of this writing. Scott hadn't spoken with all of them, obviously, but he does talk to a lot of people on a daily basis. Students. Parents. School staff. Principals. Teachers. District staff. Local government leaders. National education leaders. And he was sensing a trend.

The broadband question is often not as binary as *haves* and *have nots*. To those working in education and digital inclusion, those working every day in close proximity to the digital experience, know it is more nuanced.

Lauren Tavarez, Director of Digital Learning at ECISD and author of the Foreword, explains, "The struggle, initially, was two parts. Whether they had a connection or not. We had huge holes in connectivity in Odessa — you may struggle to connect even if you have a device. And a lot of what we ask kids and teachers to do in this virtual environment relies on video and image-heavy applications, and so that takes a big toll on your connection.

"But then the other side of that, was families not having a device at all, or just having a phone. Especially in March and April, many students were *trying* to engage in the learning, but it was done on their mom or dad's phone. So, these families were really limited when it came to bandwidth, and I think it also added extra frustration at a time that was already very frustrating and hard on people."

Scott recalls an awkward moment on a particular call in April 2020 with his Student Advisory Council, a group of high school students with whom he meets regularly in person (on Zoom during school shutdown). Scott was asking how they were all doing amid the new world of the pandemic and shutdown, and they were doing a roundtable of responses. One student was speaking when suddenly his internet service decided to take a break. He didn't drop off the call, though. You know when video goes into slow motion with the audio still on? The voice gets very low and slow, facial movements are delayed. In some places, like on Jimmy Kimmel, it can be humorous. But on Zoom or Teams in a relatively serious moment of sharing authentic feelings and experiences with your peers (and the district superintendent), it's awkward. Even worse, when this happens, the speaker usually doesn't know it's happening, so they just keep speaking. His fellow students did not openly mock him, but Scott could see some smirks and awkward frowns.

Scott was embarrassed, "I felt so sorry for him." Even though it obviously wasn't anything for anyone on the call to be embarrassed about. "It made me think of all of those kids, those without reliable internet, that are having this experience with their fellow students. Is the technology setting them up to be potentially scorned by their peers, to be made fun of?

"We have to do something for that kid. And all his peers. It's a human problem, not just a technology problem."

Based on anecdotes and minimal data, the unofficial hypothesis in the beginning was there was an access problem in the rural outskirts of Ector County, (i.e., there were pockets with no broadband access, slow service, spotty service for hotspots, dead zones, etc.), but that within town, there were decent enough options for high-speed home internet service. *The problem wasn't everywhere. Was it?*

Susan Crawford is a professor at Yale and Harvard Law School and author of the highly acclaimed, *Fiber: The Coming Tech Revolution – and Why America Might Miss It*. She frames the issue, "In short, even though two-thirds of Americans view internet access as a utility, we simply don't know, as a public matter, who is served at what address at what price with what service. We also have zero public information about the location of or cost to access poles, conduits, fiber routes, cell locations, and other key infrastructure that is essential to assessing gaps and efficiently targeting public funds."[3]

In this absence of credible data, Scott set out to gather a local view from multiple perspectives: households, private providers, government, and various technical experts. One form of analysis that could be pursued was the review of coverage maps of the county, showing where residential ("fixed") services were offered, (as reported by providers and collected by the FCC). In other words, heat maps showing where there was or wasn't service in towns and neighborhoods. Connected Nation, a non-profit that supports connectivity in rural communities, does an admirable job maintaining and supplementing these maps of Texas at the county level, (connectednation.org/texas). And while this information was useful as a guide, the accuracy of the FCC's data collection process has been notoriously flawed.

Historically, the data collection process administered by the FCC in the U.S. asked internet service providers (ISPs) to report where they offer service at a census-block level. The form ("Form 477") is filled out by the provider, results are collected and then reported back out, publicly. But the FCC does not audit this data. So, if a single customer has access to the provider's service in the census-block (and no one else), the provider would mark that area as served. If you are not already familiar with the issue, you can imagine the inaccuracies, conflicts, and bias this introduces to the quality of the data. The issue has plagued citizens, local planners, and government officials for years.

In July 2019, the FCC admitted the problem with relying solely on providers as the source of data. A new data collection process was proposed. "The Commission's current census-block level broadband deployment reporting has been an effective tool for helping the Commission target universal service support to the least-served areas of the country, but more granular data is needed to direct funding to fill the "gaps" in broadband coverage," reads the notice of proposed rulemaking by the FCC (July 11, 2019), proposing "a process to collect public input, commonly known as 'crowdsourcing,' on the accuracy of service providers' broadband maps."[4]

On March 23, 2020, President Trump signed into law the Broadband Deployment Accuracy and Technological Availability (DATA) Act, which enacted these new rules and will ideally strengthen the data collection process moving forward. Though, additional funding will be needed to execute the new process, according to former Chairman Ajit Pai, due to the higher level of effort. The coronavirus aid package passed by the House and Senate in mid-December 2020 finally authorized $65 million for this work to begin. Acting Chairwoman Rosenworcel made this a priority for the FCC in February 2021, "The Broadband Data Task Force will lead a cross-agency effort to collect detailed data and develop more precise maps about broadband availability."[5]

And while crowdsourcing and triangulation of data is great and will likely improve the accuracy of the maps in the coming years — in mid-2020, as the pandemic was shutting down the country, we were stuck with the old (overstated) data.

Kellie connected with a local architecture and

engineering firm, Parkhill, to quickly create a map with census data showing where all ECISD students resided in the county. Each student was represented with a small red dot on the map. Scott and Kellie also examined the maps showing where providers were offering fixed internet services (e.g. DSL, cable, fiber) in Ector County, indicated by a green shading of the coverage area (by Connected Nation/FCC). The images were combined and overlapped by adding a little transparency so you could see through to the student map. (This was later done with greater precision in a GIS mapping tool, 5Maps.) The red dots that remained outside the shaded areas would, in theory, show streets and neighborhoods where students lived without access to high-speed services.

The coverage maps showing where services were that offered at least 25 Mbps download speeds (the FCC benchmark for "broadband") indicated a circular mass of green covering most of the county. It was spotty and there are gaps in coverage over less populated tracts of land, but it covered the majority of areas where people currently lived. This would appear to indicate that there *wasn't* any *real* problem, right?

Many thought so. Connected Nation's data even said that 99% of Ector County households had access to services at this speed, with a few hundred households totally unserved. Except, remember that part about the *over*-estimated coverage data discussed earlier? Yeah, put that aside for a second. One local expert revealed the real reason this map showed near blanket coverage at this speed was because a fixed wireless provider with a wide coverage range had recently come to the county offering "speeds up to" 65 Mbps download. The problem was that they only publicly offered a download speed of up to 20 Mbps on their website, (for $129 a month plus tax). Higher speeds were *available upon request*.

And then we layered in the map showing where services were available of at least 100 Mbps download speed. This is the type of speed historically offered by wired providers like cable companies or fiber optics services. It is considered "fast." Some might suggest this is more than any one person usually needs. But consider for a moment a family of five with two adults working from home and three students attending remote learning Zoom sessions and streaming video throughout the day — it's about right for a family. This is not a mobile plan. These are households of people sharing a single connection; sometimes it is a compound or other land area with multiple dwellings, that might be serving the streaming and surfing needs of a dozen people. Now, that is not typical — the average number of people in a household in Ector County is 3 — but it isn't uncommon. The bandwidth necessary to run multiple applications on multiple devices in a home can add up quickly, especially in a shutdown. And that is just considering the present day.

Dr. Christopher Ali, associate professor at the University of Virginia and author of *Farm Fresh Broadband*, put it simply of the current threshold of 25 Mbps: "It is outdated." In his book, he analyzes the promise and the failure of national rural broadband policy in the United States that, among other things, has relied on this antiquated figure to allocate federal funds to grant applicants that can meet that mark. This leads the federal government to subsidize ISPs whose technologies simply won't endure for long.

When planning a community solution to meet all households' needs, should a planning team consider *average* household sizes? Do you benchmark the download speeds of *today*? A "Friday Night Lights" football metaphor for this outlook would be like approaching the end of an overtime game trailing by three points — you're marching down the field and into the opponents' territory. Time is running out. Do you go for the tie game by attempting a field goal, or go for the win with a touchdown? "Hello!?" legendary coach Herm Edwards would exclaim, "You play to win the game." Download speeds and bandwidth needs are not going down. In fact, they have been going up 50% per year for high-end users since the 1980s, according to Jakob Nielsen and his Law of Internet Bandwidth. Others have it pegged closer to 20% to 30% per year, but no one has it going down. Cisco predicts the average download speed for broadband in North America to be 142 Mbps (110 Mbps Wi-Fi speed) by 2023 in its *Annual Internet Report*.[6]

At the time of this writing, many have already called for 100 Mbps to be the new FCC benchmark for "broadband," and I predict it will be redefined in 2022. If not redefined by the FCC, perhaps heavily influenced by the final rules of the Infrastructure Investment and Jobs Act. When voting to approve the latest 25 Mbps benchmark in 2015, FCC Commissioner (now acting Chairwoman) Jessica Rosenworcel said, "I think our new threshold should be 100 Mbps. I think anything short of that shortchanges our children, our future, and our new digital economy."[7]

The reason this is important at a federal level is that billions in grant funding is (and will be) allocated to ISPs to build service that meets this minimum threshold for "broadband," as mandated in the grant requirements.

For example, the Rural Digital Opportunity Fund, a grant program of the FCC, will be distributing $20.4 billion over the next decade to such broadband providers. In other words, the lower the "broadband" threshold, the more providers there will be in the market that will get federal funding to deploy inadequate service.

Back in Ector County, when the map showing where providers offered the faster services (100 Mbps+) was overlaid with the student map, significantly more red dots appeared before our eyes. Huge pockets, entire neighborhoods, streets, areas just not offered a "fast" service.

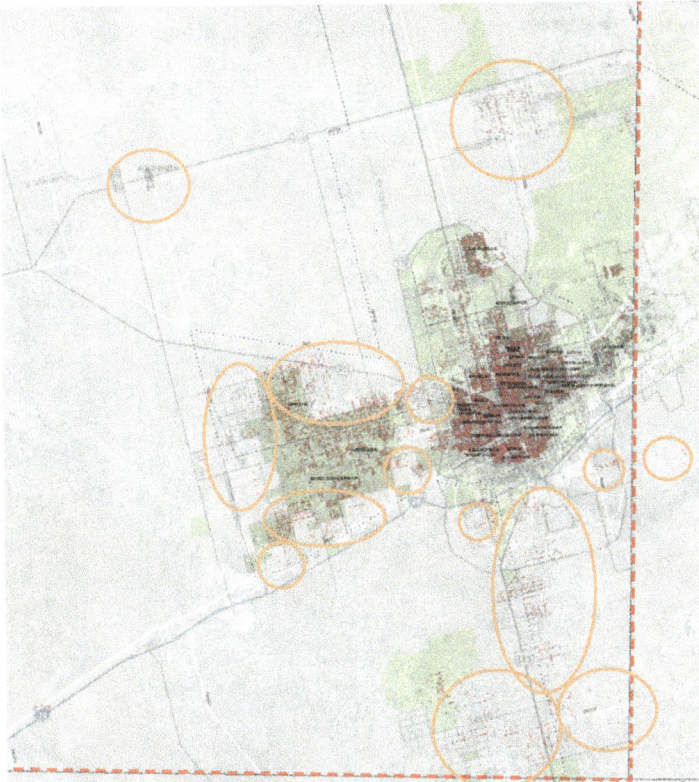

Figure 1: ECISD students (Small dots) in Areas Without Access to Fixed Services at Speeds of 100 Mbps or Better

Downtown Odessa and West Odessa were largely shaded green (meaning offered high-speed service). But there was only a sparse shading of green outside Odessa in towns like Pleasant Farms, and none in Goldsmith, Texas. (And, remember the *over-estimated* nature of the data?) This was not a revelation, exactly. The rural broadband gap is well documented. But this particular map showed Scott specifically which students in Ector County were at real risk of not having reliable internet in the home during the shutdown.

It struck a chord. It's Scott's mission in life to remove systemic obstacles like these from his students' individual experiences. Something had to be done.

Chapter 3

THE VOICE OF THE PEOPLE

*The coronavirus has exacerbated the already press-
ing need for rural communities to have reliable
phone and internet service. It is essential to take
proactive steps immediately to ensure rural Texans
have access to telework and essential services, such
as remote learning and telemedicine.*
— Brooks Landgraf,
Texas State Representative (R-Odessa)[1]

*Most residents would say there's not good options for
internet service [in Ector County].*
— Anonymous Ector County community leader

MAPS OF SELF-REPORTED ISP coverage was one thing,
but what was the word on the street? What were the
residents of Ector County saying about their home internet service (or lack thereof)? Especially, those on the
outskirts of Odessa?

Conducting a community survey in the throes of a
global pandemic, trying especially to reach those without internet access, is a challenge, to say the least. For-
tunately, the Midland Odessa Transportation Alliance
(MOTRAN), in partnership with Connected Nation and

the Odessa Development Corporation (ODC), had conducted a survey of Ector County residents in west and south Odessa as to the status of their home internet in the summer of 2019. While not the whole county, it was a good start, aimed at those most likely to be disconnected. Their survey was designed to engage individuals who may not have internet access and so was primarily conducted via paper and word of mouth. The project was able to capture survey responses from 260 residents of West and south Odessa, which yielded authentic insights into what rural customers were really experiencing.

The results, in short, showed dissatisfaction with these residents' existing services. Many said there were not any broadband services offered in their neighborhood. Or that what was offered was too expensive and they couldn't afford it. According to data compiled, those that could afford services felt the speed was too slow, and a whopping 99% of respondents indicated they were interested in better options. Nearly one in four respondents (with service) paid over $100 per month for their service, while the average was just shy of $80 per month.

Those that did not have service in their home indicated essentially two barriers to access:

(1) no options were offered where they lived (58%)

(2) they could not afford the options that were available (35%)

The root of the problem was multi-faceted.

Early on in the pandemic, mobile hotspots were in high demand and hard to get, but the district was able to purchase some for students from their local Education Service Center (ESC18). Soon thereafter, the TEA and Operation Connectivity would provide funds to purchase

1,000 additional hotspots (and iPads/Chromebooks) with two-year data plans, almost all of which were distributed in summer 2020. Scott and Kellie liked the idea of getting the Verizon hotspot devices, called Mi-Fi, to those students on the go, between multiple households, etc.— but also hoped they could reach some of those families without options where they lived.

Lauren Tavarez and her team decided to test the devices in the field before committing to it as a solution. They drove out to a select group of eligible families' addresses and ran a speed test using the Mi-Fi connection from the street. "The connection wasn't great," Lauren remembers. "And I start to wonder, you get 5 devices on that at the same time doing Google Meets with the teachers... probably not." The Mi-Fi connection relies on close proximity to a Verizon cell tower and there are a lot of Verizon towers in Ector County (more than the other wireless providers), but they aren't everywhere. Maps of cell tower installations at the time showed none to the south in Pleasant Farms, for example.

"Even without the pandemic, broadband should be a part of the learning process. In perpetuity. It has been for years," Scott told me. "And because of the diversity of access, it has widened gaps, and that'll exacerbate over the next several years unless we do something about it."

Another highly credible source of county-wide expertise also emerged to inform the effort: teachers' knowledge of their students.

Like most others, the district polled its families and communities in March about their general well-being, their experiences with the shift to distance learning, and their access to resources. Law enforcement officers were even sent out to the homes of families who did not respond, to share information on the district's remote learning strategy, including the paper-based option. The survey showed that, across the district, younger students were bored, and older students were stressed in those early days of wave one.

In May, after months of remote teaching and learning, Scott and Kellie decided to poll all of ECISD's teachers, asking them to estimate the reliability of their students' home internet connection. Schools were about to close for the summer. Because they had spent the spring online teaching their students, the teachers were in a unique position to perform the exercise. They were extremely well-versed in which of their students had been attending class (or not), dropping their connections off of Zoom calls (or not), experiencing frozen screens (or not), having audio issues (or not), submitting assignments (or not), and just based on what the students were telling them, generally. This was part of remote teaching. It had become a part of their job to know these facts.

There was really one question to ask. For each student, how often do they seem to have reliable home internet connectivity? The possible responses were "always," "most of the time," "sometimes," "rarely," or "never." If Scott and Kellie knew which students and families didn't have reliable access across the county, they could look at where they lived and representative patterns might emerge as to which geographies and neighborhoods were truly dealing with an internet access issue.

Kellie led the outreach campaign to communicate the survey to all ECISD teachers, with the hopes of accounting for the majority of students. She sent emails.

She made phone calls. She appealed to hearts and minds. She went into "bulldog" mode, as David framed it. The survey was distributed to teachers on the Monday of the last week school was in session in the 2019-2020 school year. The teachers had five days — and they responded.

In the end, the survey responses accounted for 55% of Ector County students with all schools represented. The goal of capturing data on the majority of students was achieved.

The results of the data, though, were alarming.

Chapter 4
THE PROBLEM IS NOT ONLY RURAL

In conversations with local civic and education leaders as well as economic development professionals in areas of similar size around the state, it was consistently noted that one of the most important improvements that could be made is to significantly enhance broadband availability. Universal broadband internet access to the extent possible would greatly enhance the ability for remote work and education during periods of time when social distancing may be required. In addition, it would increase efficiency in the workplace once the current situation has passed.
— Ray Perryman,
economist, The Perryman Group[1]

This is not just a rural problem, it's a rural and urban problem. And sometimes it's deployment, but sometimes it's also affordability. And I think that's something we don't talk enough about in Washington because we are always talking about, What can we do to a lay fiber and build out networks? But cost matters. If we really want to get 100% of our households online, and I would argue that that's what we

need to do, then we're going to also have to talk about affordability.
— Acting FCC Chairwoman Jessica Rosenworcel[2]

THOUGH NOT ALL students were accounted for in the survey, a significant portion of teachers and students in each of the district's schools was represented and so the results were analyzed. Teachers that responded had estimated one in five ECISD students "rarely" or "never" had reliable internet service at home in the spring of 2020.

Thirty-nine percent (39%) of students accounted for in the survey 'sometimes,' 'rarely,' or 'never' had reliable internet access at home. Assuming the survey results are representative, one in ten students just never connected that spring after schools shut down—in Ector County, that is over three thousand kids.

There are many reasons why a student might not be able to connect to their remote class other than simply not having internet at home. Language, literacy, finances, technology access and individual family situations all can play a role. A shift towards more equitable learning experiences requires a laser-like focus on the barriers to access and adoption for all students. Having high-speed internet access is no guarantee of winning the game. But not having it guarantees you don't even get to play.

The locations of the students' home addresses were mapped (anonymously) and filtered on those who "rarely" or "never" had service. ECISD subscribes to a suite of analytics tools, called Forecast5, which includes a powerful mapping application, *5Maps*. Whitney West at Forecast5 has a passion for working with school districts across the country to help them answer key questions and solve problems using GIS data. With the help of 5Maps, she often guides her clients in analyzing the geography of, say, an entire community of students instantly zooming in to specific neighborhoods, applying other layers and filters (based on our survey questions), and then taking a snapshot of the results for further analysis.

We imported our survey data of the teachers' estimates of student access into the 5Maps tool. It would show us where the students lived who sometimes, rarely, or never had reliable connectivity. This would potentially point to the neighborhoods most in need of infrastructure, and also hint at the root cause of the problem. What we saw when we reviewed the data for the first time with Whitney was initially a bit mind-blowing. There were some students in the more rural geographies of the county, but there were also *thousands* scattered around Odessa proper. Downtown. North of town. South of town. The problem was manifesting basically *everywhere* people lived. Not just in the rural areas.

Scott wasn't surprised.

He knew from the beginning that this wasn't just a question of geographic gaps in the ISPs' coverage. As superintendent of the county's school system, he knew that 56% of families in his district were economically disadvantaged.

There was an access problem. But there was also an *adoption* problem.

As described by Connected Nation, broadband *access* refers to the infrastructure that enables a high-speed internet connection. This is the network that is often built and maintained by an ISP or backhaul provider.

But broadband *adoption* is the "the choice made by a resident, business, or institution to embrace and use broadband and its related technologies." Embedded in this *choice*, is the capacity of the individual to afford and pay for the service. If they can't, they don't.

Broadband *adoption* will not take place without access to a high-speed service. But even with access, adoption may not follow. In other words, you may live in a populous area where fiber or cable are wired directly to your apartment and offered to you at a monthly rate. And those services may deliver perfectly adequate speeds to meet your needs. But if that internet service costs a hundred dollars a month and you're struggling to pay bills, you may be forced to make choices and prioritize funds for other necessities.

The problem wasn't just a lack of fixed options for customers — it was a lack of *affordable*, high-speed options. Everywhere.

The end of year survey effort was extremely helpful in that it had captured what teachers were observing, and it had reinforced Scott's understanding of the problem. But it also raised the question of more specifics. *If they didn't have service, why not? How many families did not have high-speed service? What kinds of service did households actually have? Did it meet their needs?*

A survey of all families in the district would be needed.

Chapter 5
FOLLOW THE MONEY

That [some 80 million Americans can only get high-speed broadband service from one provider] is quite intentional on the part of cable operators. These companies are extracting rent from Americans based on their monopoly positions.
— Susan Crawford,
Professor at Harvard and Yale Law Schools[1]

The United States has an internet access problem, especially in rural areas. The existing program to extend broadband has become a corporate entitlement for incumbent telephone companies. At the same time, the United States has an internet affordability problem. Too many low-income Americans cannot afford broadband internet access.
— Tom Wheeler, former FCC Chairman[2]

"IF BUILDING BROADBAND IN rural communities was easy, we would not have a digital divide in our country," said Shirley Bloomfield, CEO of the Rural Broadband Association (NTCA), in 2018.[3]

Home internet providers deliver a valuable service. In most cases, they charge a fee for this service. Those that don't charge a fee to the end user are likely to be public hotspots. But most ISPs charge a fee for service in the home. And not only that, but they target construction of their network infrastructure in neighborhoods where they are guaranteed to collect a significant amount of subscriber fees. The profit-driven, of course, refer to this as return on investment (ROI). *But what about the neighborhoods that aren't easy to build for and don't guarantee a significant ROI for the provider?*

Shirley Bloomfield continues, "the business case for bringing broadband to rural America is difficult because of the steep cost of deploying robust technologies in huge swaths of low-density countryside."

So, it's not exactly about *ease* from an effort standpoint — it's about money. Of course, higher effort leads to higher costs. But from an engineering and construction standpoint, the work is straightforward in an underdeveloped area. Not *easy*; but feasible. Dozens of private companies often exist in any particular region to provide the construction service. Electric utilities assets can be leveraged in partnerships. But a project to build a new high-performance network historically takes a significant amount of effort and time. The coming years will also see a rise in the cost of network parts and labor.

"The economics of linear density tell us it is commercially unviable to deploy network infrastructure at affordable consumer rates in a rural environment without some form of subsidy, whether internal or external," described James Stegeman upon release of a report he authored in 2018 on the subject, produced for USTelecom and NTCA.[4]

By "external" subsidy, Mr. Stegeman is referring to large capital investments from a government or other entity, like a grant, to fund the construction or expansion of a network into unserved geographies, (which the ISP is not willing to front on their own). But, as explicitly stated above, the ISPs are usually willing to accept a generous gift ("subsidy") to finance the construction of the infrastructure so they can offer service in the area. They would just prefer not to put up the investment themselves, because the return isn't there in the near-term. So, let someone else assume that risk. This behavior is actually quite predictable: if there's no near-term profit in it for them, the commercial ISP won't build a network there.

If this seems wrong — if it feels like it's perpetuating inequities against already marginalized groups; if it reeks of discrimination — then you might classify this *a problem.* Christopher Ali, among others, refers to this condition as a *market failure* in his 2019 opinion piece in the *New York Times;* and a "policy failure" that we do not have a national rural broadband plan.[5]

And market failures can happen anywhere.

In 2016, AT&T was accused of "digital redlining" in Dallas (and similarly in Cleveland in 2017; and in Detroit in 2017) as highlighted in the National Digital Inclusion Alliance's report aptly titled, *AT&T's Digital Redlining,* and corroborated by research conducted by Dr. Brian Whitacre, a professor in the Agricultural Economics Department at Oklahoma State University who specializes in research on broadband access and use. Dr. Whitacre illustrates both the case and what *digital redlining* is in his summary: "The analysis for Dallas demonstrates that AT&T has withheld fiber-enhanced broadband improvements from most Dallas neighborhoods with high poverty rates, relegating them to Internet access services which are vastly inferior to the services enjoyed by their counterparts nearby in the higher-income Dallas suburbs. ... Because the patterns revealed by this analysis result from a decade of deliberate infrastructure investment decisions, I argue that they constitute strong evidence of a policy and practice of "digital redlining" by AT&T — i.e. income-based discrimination against residents of lower-income urban neighborhoods in the types of broadband service AT&T offers, and in the company's investment in improved service."[6]

Under 47 USC 151, the Communications Act of 1934 establishes: "For the purpose of regulating interstate and foreign commerce in communication by wire and radio so as to make available, so far as possible, to all the people of the United States, without discrimination on the basis of race, color, religion, national origin, or sex, a rapid, efficient, Nation-wide, and world-wide wire and radio communication service with adequate facilities at reasonable charges." The AT&T example above is just one case of one provider. There are many more, and they are reported to the FCC every year. It is illustrative of how the private sector strategizes the construction of their network infrastructure. New York City had to sue Verizon in 2020 (and it won) to complete construction of fiber service in low-income neighborhoods.[7] There are also countless other cases of providers over-charging their customers, both with hidden fees and high rates.

Around the time AT&T was accused of digital redlining in Dallas, Kellie was noticing steadily increasing fees charged by AT&T for the fiber optic service provided to ECISD schools. ECISD schools had been wired for internet connectivity for quite some time, and their provider was AT&T going back almost twenty years. AT&T was not the only available provider at the time that could serve high-speed access to the schools in the county, but the costs of switching to other providers would be high due to certain equipment under lease. As the fees kept getting hiked up, Kellie and others in the community became increasingly frustrated. And they felt powerless. That is, until the district decided to take matters into their own hands and partner with someone else to build new fiber optic lines to all the schools. The project took several years and was wrapping up as the pandemic hit.

Call it monopoly. Call it "digital redlining." Say it is the product of the "economics of linear density." Call it discrimination. Call it the "free market." Call it what you will — but in home broadband, it's a big problem for 8-year-old Myra trying to join a Zoom call with her teacher. And it's a problem for 53-year-old Robert, an oil rig operator, trying to apply and interview for a job when he has no internet in the home. This is the prevailing home internet delivery model for most U.S. residents: the commercial ISP. But there are other delivery models out there — for example, municipal, cooperative, and public-private partnerships — which we'll explore more in Chapter 8.

The internet certainly isn't the first time in history that the expansion of technology needed a boost from outside the private sector, as we'll review next.

Chapter 6

HISTORY RHYMES

Great discoveries and improvements invariably involve the cooperation of many minds.
— Alexander Graham Bell

History doesn't repeat itself, but it rhymes.
— Mark Twain

ELECTRICITY AND THE TELEPHONE were once nascent innovations, in the early startup stages of their inevitable adoption across the globe. At the start, only the privileged or resourceful were able to get it, and access was far from ubiquitous as it is today. We often forget this. We take for granted the illumination of a space we can summon with a flick of the index finger. There are amazing parallels in the history and expansion of these utilities with what we are witnessing today in the expansion of internet services to the home.

On January 28, 1878, two years after Alexander Graham Bell was awarded a patent on his most famous invention, the world's first commercial telephone exchange opened for business in New Haven, Connecticut, under license from the Bell Telephone Company. George Coy, Herrick Frost, and Walter Lewis formed what came to be known as the Southern New England Telephone Company. Growth and expansion of telephone access continued almost exclusively in urban areas of the east coast U.S. for decades. There eventually became a focus on the "long lines," connecting first between New York and Philadelphia, the precursor to long-distance service. There was not a targeted effort to reach all households until Theodore Vail became president of the Bell Company in 1907.

Vail coined the phrase "universal service," a concept and term that survive to this day. In its annual report in 1911, AT&T "believed that the telephone system should be universal, interdependent and intercommunicating, affording opportunity for any subscriber of any exchange to communicate with any other subscriber of any other exchange." Sounds pretty good. But the author of the report, conjuring images of universality and *"the electrical transmission of intelligence,"* continues, "It is not believed that this can be accomplished by separately controlled or distinct systems nor that there can be competition in the accepted sense of competition.

"It is believed that all this can be accomplished to the reasonable satisfaction of the public with its acquiescence, under such control and regulation as will afford the public much better service at less cost than any competition or government-owned monopoly could permanently afford and at the same time be self-sustaining."

The comparison to *government-owned monopoly* is ironic — but *self-sustaining* they were.

A U.S. map of the Bell Telephone System in 1910 available online shows a westward expansion in progress. Jennifer Onion writes in *Slate*, "The map shows Bell's market penetration in 1910, three years after Vail took over. Some rural areas — Oklahoma, Iowa, northern and eastern Texas — are surprisingly well-covered, while others in the Southeast remain empty." The first transcontinental phone call, from New York to Los Angeles, would not be placed until 1914.[1]

But, as Onion notes, towns in western and southern Texas appear less connected on the map. Keeping in mind the ongoing expansion, Texas almost resembled a picture of haves and have-nots in 1910. One can see the map of telephone lines in the David Rumsey map collection online (davidrumsey.com), and can even zoom in to the local level. Lines can be seen extending out from Dallas and Santa Fe to reach Odessa and El Paso. But only barely. The line does not extend past Odessa to the south or west. The towns to the south and southwest, such as Pecos and Fort Stockton, were not connected yet. Odessa was right on the edge of the frontier. The last mile. The end of the line. The telephone had been invented almost 35 years prior.

AT&T would of course face multiple antitrust lawsuits in the 20th century, notoriously settled in 1913 and 1982. "The first Bell Monopoly was a service for the rich, operating mainly in cities in the East, with limited long distance capacity," writes Tim Wu in *The Master Switch*. "The idea of a mass telephone service connecting everyone else was still decades away."[2]

The "Kingsbury Commitment" was a piece of the 1913 settlement that would require AT&T to share its long lines with local independent providers' services, referred to as "interconnecting," thereby lessening its stranglehold on the infrastructure side. This regulation may well have changed the course of U.S. telecommunications history allowing for a flourishing of competition had it not been effectively repealed eight years later by the Willis Graham Act of 1921. While progress towards connectivity would continue, and most towns and municipalities would eventually be connected, the languid pace of progress and lack of coverage became a problem for farmers and rural residents in the early 20th century. Opening a business, like a factory, simply wasn't in the cards without access to telephone or electricity.

When Bell's second patent expired in 1894, thousands of small, locally based telephone companies and cooperatives jumped into the game. Many called themselves the "Independents." Wu describes, "They saw a different world, in which the telephone was made cheaper and more common, a tool of mass communications, and an aid in daily life. They intuited that the telephone's paramount value was not as a better version of the telegraph or a more efficient means of commerce, but as the first social technology. As one farmer captured it in 1904, 'With a telephone in the house comes a new companionship, new life, new possibilities, new relationships, and attachments for the old farm by both old and young.'"[3] Around this time, about 6,000 "independent" phone companies begin operating in the U.S., quickly growing to 20,000 or so.[4] All-out competition ensued, with independents competing with AT&T in some markets and with each other in others. But by 1940, due to the struggling economy, many farmers and rural residents simply had to give up their telephones, devastating the financials of many of the independents.

The telephone divide would widen during the Depression, and another technology that would one day become ubiquitous was slowly rolling out across the country, as well: electricity to the home.

Going into the Depression, nine out of 10 rural homes were without electricity. This was a major problem that hampered the economic opportunities of rural residents. The first official action of the federal government to support rural electrification came with the passage of the Tennessee Valley Authority (TVA) Act in May 1933. This act authorized the TVA Board to construct power lines to serve "farms and small villages that are not otherwise supplied with electricity at reasonable rates."[5]

Providing federal assistance to accomplish rural electrification as a concept gained ground rapidly when President Franklin Roosevelt took office and signed an Executive Order 7037 in 1935 establishing the Rural Electrification Administration (REA). The legislation was passed a year later and a lending program got underway. The lending program would, in theory, direct funding to private electric companies to build out the necessary infrastructure in rural areas. The process for applying for loans was launched, but it soon became clear to REA officials that private utility companies were not all that interested in using federal loan funds to serve sparsely populated rural areas. Very few applications were submitted by private companies. Remember the *economics of linear density*? Loan applications from farmer-based cooperatives, however, poured in. It was at this point that many realized electric cooperatives would be the predominant entities to bring electricity to the countryside.[6]

But what exactly is a cooperative? "Co-ops" are member-owned. This means they don't have a single owner, they aren't a public entity, and they aren't owned by shareholders. If you pay for the service and any associated member fees, you are an owner. You have a vote in the appointment of the Board of Directors, and everyone has one vote. Revenue and profits are generated, but profits are not paid out to owners — they are invested back in the co-op or used to refund member fees for that year. The priority and motivation shift from the bottom line to the goal of simply providing high quality service. Some refer to this as "services-first design."[7] In the broadband industry, this typically equates to high-speed, low subscriber cost, and quality technical support. The mission of one broadband co-op discussed in Chapter 8 is "To provide reliable advanced communication services with superior customer care that enhances communities, economic development, healthcare, education, and public safety."[8]

Today, about 99% of the nation's farms have electric service. Much of the electricity outside urban areas comes from locally owned electric cooperatives that got their start by borrowing funds from the REA to build lines and provide service on a not-for-profit basis. REA is now the Rural Utilities Service, or RUS, and is part of the U.S. Department of Agriculture. Christopher Mitchell of the Institute for Local Self-Reliance writes, "Universal electricity required some 4,000 municipal electric departments and nearly 1,000 rural electric cooperatives. And it worked. Not because municipal networks and cooperatives are magical, but because they have the right incentives."[9]

Back to telephony. The Communications Act of 1934 discussed in the previous chapter also created the Federal Communications Commission (FCC), and charged it with ensuring the provision of quality telephone service to all Americans at reasonable rates, among other objectives. However, rural telephone service availability and quality remained poor throughout the early half of the

20th century until low-interest loans to companies and cooperatives became available as part of the REA loan program in 1949.[10]

It would seem the private sector position of a lack of ROI and the need for "subsidies" to deploy in rural areas, discussed in Chapter 5, follows the historical pattern. Christopher Ali writes, "when it comes to rural connectivity, private companies refuse to connect sparsely populated communities because there is not return on investment—the very definition of market failure. To remedy this in telecommunications, Congress established a policy goal of "universal service," first with telephony in the 1934 Communications Act, then electricity in the 1944 Agriculture Organic Act, and later with "advanced telecommunications" in the 1996 Telecommunications Act."[11]

On its website at https://www.fcc.gov/general/universal-service, the FCC transparently explains the history of *universal* telephone service: "The Federal Communications Commission was created by the Communications Act of 1934. Universal service was one of the core mandates of that legislation, the purpose of which included making available ... to all the people of the United States ... a rapid, efficient, Nation-wide, and world-wide wire and radio communication service with adequate facilities at reasonable charges."

They continue, "In 1934, telephone service was considered to be a 'natural monopoly,' a service best delivered by one company rather than two or more competitors. The U.S. government allowed AT&T, then the monopoly provider, to operate in a non-competitive environment in most areas of the country in exchange for the federal and state government regulation of price and service quality.

In areas that AT&T did not provide service, small companies, including cooperatives owned by residents of the local community, provided phone service. The concept of universal service evolved over the decades to mean the development of an infrastructure that provides telephone service to all consumers at a reasonable price."

Fast forward through the monopoly years to the 1990s. The Telecommunications Act of 1996 finally declared the phone lines as public infrastructure, requiring the telecommunications companies to share (interconnect) the lines, allowing more entrants into the competitive field. And since most internet service was provided over phone lines in the late '90s, (i.e. dial-up), it seemed like an era of great competition was upon us. But like the Graham Hawley Act of 1921 would do to the Kingsbury Commitment, deregulation sentiment swept through a post-9/11 world following the dot-com bust, and in 2002 the FCC under the Bush administration essentially declared cable internet service not a telecommunications service, and so not beholden to the regulations around this sharing of infrastructure. This was upheld by the U.S. Supreme Court in 2005 — or rather, the Supreme Court issued no opinion, deferring to the interpretation of the FCC. This is why, today, you probably live in an area with only one good choice of cable internet service.

"That's when everything came tumbling down," explains Gigi Sohn, Distinguished Fellow at Georgetown Law and a Benton Senior Fellow and Public Advocate, on the EFF podcast, "The so-called free market in broadband was allowed to reign. And what you got, under both Democrats and Republicans, was intense consolidation, regional monopolies, and guess what happens with concentration of monopoly? High prices."[12]

The Telecommunications Act of 1996 also created a grant program, the Universal Service Fund (USF), which was designed to be funded by providers and would direct support to four program areas:

- *Connect America Fund* (formally known as High-Cost Support) for expanding access in rural areas
- *Lifeline* for low-income subscribers of telephone service, a sponsored service (subsidy), including initiatives to expand phone service for residents of Tribal lands
- Expanded access for schools and libraries (*E-rate*)
- Rural Health Care

As a historical question, who is truly responsible for connecting all of the U.S. to telephone service in the 20th century — Ma Bell, cooperatives, local providers, or the government — will continue on as spirited debate for telecom geeks indefinitely. I would contend all had a truly significant role to play.

"One thing we know, however," writes Susan Crawford in *Fiber*, "is that humans have never preferred less connectivity at higher prices."[13]

But, back to cooperatives and the present day. Today, many telephone and electric cooperatives have logically expanded their offerings to include a high-speed broadband service, a lucrative product they can often add to their portfolio given a relatively moderate investment in the infrastructure. Telephone providers are in a unique position to provide DSL service, which is delivered over phone lines (though it is in the process of being phased out). And electric cooperatives, which need distributed connectivity for their operations, can often extend the infrastructure they build (typically fiber optics) as an internet service to a nearby household. They are already well positioned to leverage their existing resources and capacity to maintain power lines, conduits, and other infrastructure.

The story we are told of cooperatives in the 20th century was, out of a necessity, to connect those that the private sector would not, and to spur economic development, local organizations could step up to fill the gap. An alternative perspective is that cooperatives were more accurately launched by wealthy elites wanting to connect or power their remote lake houses. But whether catalyzed by privilege or the simple demand of the unserved (or both), cooperatives have historically worked well for the subscriber. Most broadband industry experts today agree that for home internet service, cooperatives typically offer better quality of service than their private sector competitors. More on specific examples of this in Chapter 8.

History is, of course, a wealth of knowledge containing the personalities, organizations and decisions that shaped the present-day world. Historian Jon Meacham says, "The past always seems somehow more golden, more serious, than the present. We tend to forget the partisanship of yesteryear, preferring to re-imagine our history as a sure and steady march toward greatness." But history can be a teacher, as many have said, for those that take the time to learn. And when we look closely, that's when we realize that lessons can be borrowed, prior causes and effects showcased under the spotlight of hindsight. Patterns and cycles emerge, leading possibly, through thoughtful

analysis, to the ability to predict the best path forward.
And then, some guy starts launching rockets into space.

Chapter 7
2021: A SPACEX ODYSSEY

*Space is for everybody. It's not just for a few people
in science or math, or for a select group of astro-
nauts. That's our new frontier out there, and it's
everybody's business to know about space.*
— Christa McAuliffe

*Sending this tweet through space via Starlink satel-
lite. Whoa, it worked!!*
— Elon Musk

THE HISTORY OF THE INTERNET, especially broadband
service, is so relatively short, we are still witnessing its
expansion. As a society, we still haven't connected every
home that needs or wants to be connected. As Shirley
Bloomfield stated earlier, there would appear not to be
an economic incentive for the private sector to do so.
But this is based on the assumption of said private sector operating a fixed (or *wired*) network that needs to
be *constructed* everywhere there are people living and
working, and all of the resources and effort that go along
with that. Even wireless networks still need to connect to
something that is wired. This is often called "backhaul."
Susan Crawford, in *Fiber*, sets the global context,

"In the United States, we have fiber optic cables between cities, called "long-haul" or "backbone" lines.
And within any metro area of significant size, there are
"middle mile" or "business data services" fiber optic
lines. These cables often connect to telephone poles or
other network elements, but don't go all the way to retail
customers' premises. What Korea, Japan, Hong Kong,
China, Singapore, and the Nordic countries have that
the rest of the world does not are fiber optic cables running physically, directly, into neighborhoods, homes,
and businesses in both rural and urban areas — the so-
called "last mile" network."[1]

The "last mile" has been difficult to build out in
many places where terrain or remote geography introduce construction obstacles. But what if you could beam
a high-speed wireless signal from space? (Technically,
from a backhaul line connected to a base station on the
ground beamed up to the satellite in orbit and then down
to the home.) Would that preclude the need for all this
expensive infrastructure construction on earth? Internet
service offered by satellite TV providers like Dish and
DirecTV has been around for decades. It has not exactly been in the *broadband* category historically, because
the speeds offered have only recently approached the 25
Mbps threshold. And weather is a problem.

Elon Musk founded SpaceX in 2002 with the goal
of innovating space travel. What has become almost as
big a story is *Starlink*, a program of SpaceX, which secured licensing by the FCC to deploy tens of thousands
of low-Earth orbit (LEO) satellites (a constellation) capable of transmitting broadband internet virtually anywhere on earth. "Low-Earth orbit" is exactly what it
sounds like, a lower flight path for the satellites so that

they can transmit signals to the home faster than traditional satellite internet service, (the resulting effect is referred to as "latency" — *low latency* is good). Many of SpaceX's launch missions in recent years included the deployment of these satellites.

Starlink doesn't broadcast the signal from satellite to the home directly but works with a base station, or transceiver, on the ground to connect to the internet (through backhaul). Subscribers need to install a dish-like device (dubbed "Dishy McFlatface" by Mr. Musk) outside their home with a clear view of the sky, which will connect to the satellite via the base station on one end and be wired to their router on the subscriber end, creating their home Wi-Fi signal. A mobile app will assist with the setup.

Sounds like a real competitor to the traditional telecommunications companies ("telcos") that offer internet service, like Comcast and Charter, right? Elon Musk doesn't really think so. The way he sees it, Starlink will be primarily serving the unserved, who were not historically customers of the telcos (by definition) and may never be due to where they resided. "Starlink is not some huge threat to telcos. I want to be super clear: it is not," Musk told the crowd at the Satellite 2020 conference in early March. Musk estimated the satellite internet market as high as $30 billion a year, a relatively small percentage of the total internet services market, globally.

He continued, "So Starlink will effectively serve the 3 or 4% hardest-to-reach customers for telcos, or people who simply have no connectivity right now. Or the connectivity is really bad. So I think it will be actually helpful and take a significant load off the traditional telcos."[2] Starlink's stated mission on their website is to provide "high speed broadband internet to locations where access has been unreliable, expensive, or completely unavailable."

Starlink and other LEOs essentially won't have to "build" the last mile in a traditional sense. Or, another way to say it is, they are building a new last mile service.

SpaceX and Musk have a long-standing relationship with the state of Texas. There's the rocket test facility in McGregor, Texas, north of Austin. There's the launch-pad in Boca Chica, in south Texas near South Padre Island, (as close to the faster-spinning equator as possible to give rockets a boost on launch). And, at the time of writing, Tesla was building the Cybertruck Gigafactory on 2,100 acres east of Austin, and SpaceX was building a factory to manufacture Dishy McFlatface and other consumer devices, like the router, also in the Austin area. With rockets being launched regularly and humans being put into space, SpaceX had obviously proven they could get stuff done.

The only problem with Starlink in the summer of 2020 was it was unproven. To David Irwin, as we began researching long-term solutions for the county, Starlink seemed like just a distracting, shiny object. It hadn't yet been deployed commercially, and its goal of high speeds and low latency relied on the deployment of tens of thousands of satellites — at the time, SpaceX had deployed in the hundreds. Satellite internet, more generally, was historically, notoriously, beachball-spinningly slow. It suffered from latency challenges, with the signal having to travel too far to ever achieve high speeds. It was unclear exactly if the low-Earth orbit would solve this. David and Paul Donovan, a veteran program manager at ExxonMobile (now retired) advising the Permian

Strategic Partnership (PSP) on broadband strategy, had questions.

Starlink staff gave a presentation to the PSP, a coalition of 20 energy companies in the region, in spring 2020. David attended, and asked the Starlink team about the latency challenge. They responded that they had made some significant technological advances that would overcome the "whole physics and math thing," as David put it. It was hard for Starlink to even provide accurate figures on speed, because not all of the satellites were deployed, and faster speed depended on more satellites being deployed. So, they couldn't even test the service for high speeds in a realistic environment yet. David hesitated in bringing the option to Scott and Kellie as a realistic solution.

Did the idea of Starlink align with the district's goal of expanded access for its students? Yes. *Did the vendor seem capable?* They were launching rockets into space every few weeks, so … yes. *Could it possibly accelerate the work we're doing in trying to connect kids?* Yes. In June, David had a call with Starlink staff and decided that a pilot could have many benefits. In technology circles, a "pilot" is an experiment, of sorts. An emerging platform or service is essentially tried out with a small group to capture feedback on the experience from participants to inform whether the solution should scale further. The decision to implement the solution for the broader community is made later, or not at all. This feedback is also typically valuable to the product team building it. A *pilot*, while an experiment of sorts, was low-risk to Scott and the county and could get a real solution in some unserved homes quickly. It could be offered to families for free with philanthropists' support, and feedback could be gathered on how well it worked. There were a lot of optics focused on whether this could actually work, from philanthropies to media to government. On May 30, 2020, SpaceX had successfully launched the Falcon 9 Dragon crew into space, headed for the International Space Station. Scott was well aware of SpaceX's results. He was ready and willing to give it a try. And he knew a few good-hearted folks who might be willing to pick up the check.

Kellie, David, ECISD legal staff, and Starlink staff entered into contract discussions. ECISD would be one of Starlink's first customers. Starlink charges a fee, as ISPs do, so Scott brought together a group of local organizations to invest in the one-year pilot that would bring service to 135 families — the Permian Strategic Partnership, the Moody Foundation, Grow Odessa (an economic development non-profit), and Chiefs for Change (a bipartisan network of education leaders). Starlink would later cut the cost of the site hardware for customers. Based on the mapping analysis produced, which confirmed that the area south of Odessa had generally poor or no home internet services, families in the town of Pleasant Farms, Texas, would be surveyed as to their interest in the pilot, and those interested would be invited to participate, (i.e. through a lottery if demand exceeded the pilot size). Families began receiving the service in early 2021.

On October 20, 2020, ECISD issued a statement that the district would be the first in the nation to utilize SpaceX satellites to provide home internet service for students. "We are thrilled to have this opportunity to work with committed partners like the PSP and Chiefs for Change, as well as SpaceX and its next generation internet solution to provide service for our families," Scott said at a press briefing that day. "Closing the digital divide in our community is a key element in our district's strategic plan. Ector County ISD is determined to lead this effort because we believe this is a moral imperative and simply the right work to do for our students." Governor Greg Abbott celebrated the news, tweeting, "Now that's what I call Texas partnership!"

This did not mean the problem had been solved. Starlink was still unproven in the summer of 2020. Beta testing was ongoing in the fall, and by November, speeds in those test environments were exceeding 100 Mbps download speeds in most instances. Amidst the backdrop of the pandemic, most were hoping for Starlink to succeed, namely because it could be so quickly and easily deployed to families. But it wouldn't be until the spring or summer of 2021, after residents had had some time using the service in their homes, that there would be substantial data on the reliability of the fledgling service.

Kellie and Scott's plan was not to sit around and wait. Perhaps the solution in the future would be a combination of LEO satellite technology service and something else, (i.e., a "hybrid"). Or *several* other things. The survey of Ector County households was prepared, and questions were added to gauge interest in the pilot. Research and data gathering continued, and Scott and Kellie prepared to bring the findings to a county task force that would be convened in the fall of 2020.

Because of the pandemic, David and I had not yet been able to visit Odessa at this point. Our work had all been done remotely. One day, just as the survey was being distributed to families, David was speaking with

Starlink staff and the topic of installation came up and that a clear view of the sky would be needed for Dishy McFlatface to get the signal. *There can't be a bunch of trees blocking the line of sight to the sky*, he was told. *Oh boy,* David realized this should have been something asked in the survey to identify households that might not be able to receive the signal.

After the call, David somewhat frantically called Kellie and relayed the need for pilot participants to have a clear view of the sky, thinking they may need to update the survey at the last minute. "Basically, there can't be a bunch of trees in the way."

Kellie smiled and chuckled. "Um, David," she replied, "there are no big trees in Ector County."

This is, apparently, a well-known fact to anyone that has ever been to the area. There is even a town in the county called Notrees.

Scott and Kellie even saw an opportunity in the increasing public interest and awareness SpaceX was bringing to space as a subject of science. They and ECISD Chief Innovation Officer, Jason Osborne, strategized ways to infuse SpaceX's work and video content (of rocket launches, satellite deployments, etc.) into the district's STEM curriculum. Students at Ector County's schools that want to learn more about engineering low-Earth orbit constellations will now be able to do that.

"We, as a school system, are fostering the right conditions in our community for innovation," Scott told me over Zoom one day. "And innovators will rise and provide better, more reliable, less expensive solutions for our families."

Chapter 8

BRIGHT SPOTS

The best broadband is local broadband.
— Dr. Christopher Ali,
— Associate Professor at University of Virginia

Local communities should have the opportunity to decide for themselves how to invest in their own infrastructure, including the options of working with willing incumbent carriers, creating incentives for private sector development, entering into creative public-private partnerships, or even building their own networks, if necessary or appropriate.
— Letter to FCC Chairman Wheeler in 2014,
signed by U.S. Senators Franken, Klobuchar, Markey, Blumenthal, and Booker and U.S. Representatives Doyle, Waxman, and Eshoo[1]

THERE IS A WEALTH OF literature available online in articles and reports that profile community broadband projects, both successful and unsuccessful, throughout the years.

Success is in the eye of the beholder, of course, but it is no stretch to say there are more writings on the successes than the failures. Critics will point out that this is creating a bias in the public's mind that these types of infrastructure projects inevitably end in success. However, it might be possible that there are simply far more positive outcomes than negative ones. There is certainly no shortage of reporters and writers looking for stories of failure and wastes of taxpayer funds, (even when taxpayer funds aren't used).

It is important to read both sides: the successes and the failures. They can be highly instructive to community leaders along the path of their journey.

Kellie and Scott were speaking with, reading and hearing regularly about other communities in Texas and nationally who had gotten proactive and done something about their internet affordability and access problems. There didn't seem to be a standard approach that each of them had followed, and not all were aimed at solving the same problems. Individuals, neighborhoods, businesses, school districts, and communities marginalized by the traditional ISP market were, and are, making headlines every day in attempts to expand access and adoption in their local area, typically with positive results. Were there failures? Yes. (See next chapter.) Were there risks and costs? Of course.

But Scott's general character skews towards the proactive, as these communities were getting the ball rolling on closing the divide. He believed a sustainable, long-term broadband strategy for the county could address the gaps and promote competition in the local market with the eventual effect of lower prices to make fees more affordable to households. But in no way did Scott see that path forward as his unilateral decision to make. He just wanted "a seat at the table."

The community was highly supportive of their

superintendent and was looking to him to lead them through this unprecedented time. To address the broadband problem, what Scott really wanted first was to carve out some time ("a safe space") with his peers in the county to review what other communities had done and discuss the viability of different options amongst themselves. In discussing the options and coming together on what would be best for Ector County, a strategy and long-term plan could be hatched.

Scott reached out individually to about 25 leaders in the Ector County community, inviting them to participate on a task force — they all accepted. Members included former Odessa Mayors Lorraine Perryman and David Turner, state Representative Brooks Landgraf, Paul Donovan, business and economic leaders like Chris Cole and Ray Perryman, higher education leaders, broadband experts, and other industry and community leaders. It was coined, the *ConnEctor Task Force.* (For *connecting* Ector County. Get it?)

The group was not limited to technology leaders and so, first, would need a level-setting of terminology with illustrative case studies. David, Kellie, Scott, and I researched and connected with other counties and towns that had banded together to solve their broadband woes themselves. Many kept coming up again and again, and patterns emerged. A few of the case studies were in Texas, but all were medium-sized communities, predominantly rural with some urban components, and all had compelling origin stories to tell. We called them "bright spots."

Communities that Got Themselves Connected

One of the bright spots is a telephone cooperative

in eastern Kentucky formed with federal REA funds (Chapter 5), the People's Rural Telephone Cooperative (PRTC). Formed in 1950 to provide telephone service in rural areas, PRTC partnered with four other companies to form Appalachian Wireless in the 1990s, constructing a 375-mile ring of fiber optic cable. The fiber optics infrastructure was eventually extended even farther, and can now offer 1 Gigabit per second (Gbps) speed to every home, business, and school in the two counties. You might be surprised to hear that Kentucky has at least a dozen other telephone cooperatives with similar offerings.

Ten towns in Minnesota partnered together more recently to build another mixed services offering — wireless and wired (fiber) — using the cooperative delivery model, forming *RS Fiber* (a co-op ISP). In 2015, the project began using multiple construction crews to simultaneously build out their fiber ring, connect fiber to fixed wireless towers, and build fiber to the premises (FTTP), (which means a fiber optic connection directly into the home or business). By the end of 2015, 90% of residents were covered with access to the fixed wireless service at speeds of 25 Mbps "symmetrical" (meaning same upload speed as download speed), which allowed RS Fiber to begin collecting monthly revenue and start retiring debt as soon as residents received service. In 2018, the cooperative financed the remaining construction through a bond to build the network out to the remaining farmlands. When complete, the entire network will cover 10 towns, about 600 miles and 2,500 farms. The cost was $70 million.[2]

In 2009, the Electric Power Board (EPB) of Chattanooga, Tennessee, a cooperative, began modernizing the city's electric grid and was exploring the use of smart meters on residents' homes, which would require a communications signal of some kind. City and EPB officials realized that it would be relatively simple to begin offering internet service to residents if they were going to run fiber through much of Chattanooga anyway. And so they did — but not before being sued four times by Comcast and AT&T. Long story, short: the city and EPB prevailed in court, and the City Council finally allowed EPB to take out a $169 million loan to begin building the network. Taxpayer dollars were never used despite claims made in the media campaign waged by Comcast and AT&T.[3]

In 2010, EPB lit up the newly constructed network and Chattanooga became the first city in the United States to offer 1 Gigabit per second (Gbps) service to all residents. In 2015 and 2017, EPB was the top internet service provider in *Consumer Reports* telecom ratings. The *Gig City* was born.

In Utah, 11 cities and towns joined together in 2004 to build a fiber-optics based network — UTOPIA fiber (Utah Telecommunication Open Infrastructure Agency) — the infrastructure of which could be leased out to a variety of local ISPs who could then offer service on the network, giving residents a choice of provider. This type of model is often referred to as an "open access network." And similarly, the Eastern Shore of Virginia Broadband Authority (ESVBA) is a not-for-profit public entity created to serve the residents of the eastern peninsula of Virginia. ESVBA provides connectivity and dedicated service to customers themselves but also allows any certified provider to use (lease) their network to provide services to customers, as well.

When the service is provided directly by a government entity, this is referred to as a "municipal" delivery model. It doesn't mean the service is free; it's just run by the public sector. UTOPIA, mentioned above, refers to itself as municipally owned, "a consortium of Utah cities that have united to deploy and operate state-of-the-art fiber optic networks in communities across the state," according to their website.

The first of these municipally owned open access networks was nDanville in southern Virginia, constructed in 2004. The municipal ISP's website describes its phased approach to offering services: "At its inception, the nDanville project was divided into three phases to systematically begin serving the City of Danville. The first phase was to connect area schools, providing better resources for students and teachers. The second phase, Fiber to the Business, offers greater bandwidth, speeds and accessibility to area businesses and those that locate in Danville. Service to schools and businesses is provided directly from nDanville. The third, final and current phase is Fiber to the Home, which provides infrastructure for third-party providers to offer super fast Internet connections, fiber optic television and digital VoIP telephone service."[4]

At the time of this writing, almost 20 states (depending on your legal interpretation) have laws barring municipalities from forming their own internet service and competing with traditional telecommunications providers. The existence of these laws is the result of a transparent pattern of telco lobbying. Though Texas is one of these states restricting municipal services, a community called Mont Belvieu believed they were within their rights to bring fiber to their residents, just as they would water and electricity. Mont Belvieu is a small town east of Houston, and residents had been growing increasingly impatient with a lack of high-speed internet service. A survey conducted in 2016 revealed that 60% of Mont Belvieu residents and 79% of businesses felt that local internet access wasn't adequate for their needs. Rather than ask forgiveness later, they decided to proactively address the question directly in court.

Mont Belvieu filed a petition in February 2017 in the District Court of Chambers County requesting an expedited declaratory judgment as to whether they would be able to legally fund the project and build their own network. The court considered and ruled in Mont Belveiu's favor, paving the way for the town to offer a new service, *MB Link*, to residents for internet service, (but no voice or video services, in keeping with Texas law). Attorneys for Mont Belvieu highlighted for the court that the statutory definitions of "local telephone and telecommunications" (to which the law applied) did not overlap with the definition of providing broadband through a fiber optic network, and the court agreed.[5]

In 2019, Governor Greg Abbott signed into law legislation enabling electric cooperatives to offer broadband services to customers, but municipal governments are still barred from providing broadband services to residents.

"More than 500 other communities around the country operate publicly owned internet networks. In general, these networks are cheaper, faster, and more transparent in their pricing than their private sector counterparts, despite lacking Comcast and Verizon's gigantic economies of scale," write David Elliot Berman and Victor Pickard for *Fast Company*, citing the ILSR website which tracks these types of communities.[6]

Categories of Connected Communities

These examples follow patterns. A group of people feel their neighborhoods and businesses are not adequately connected. They form a new organization to address the inequities. These people may come from different walks of life — private sector, government, concerned citizens — but the organization they form and the business model they choose is of critical importance.

The *delivery model*, as referred to in this book, is the type of organization offering the internet service. The delivery models for home broadband service in the United States are predominantly:

1. Private/commercial
2. Member-owned (a cooperative)
3. Municipal or Tribal
4. Public-Private Partnership ("P3")

The private/commercial sector delivery model is what the majority of people in the U.S. transact with today for home broadband, (e.g., Charter and Comcast). As discussed earlier, private entities are profit-driven and make investment decisions based on ROI, (not equitable distribution). Unfortunately, many community leaders and residents seem to assume this delivery model is the only real way to get internet access. Awareness of the other options is generally low in many communities, something this book is trying to change.

Municipal and cooperative models have been discussed elsewhere in this book, which brings us to the public-private delivery model option. Traditionally, a public-private partnership (or a "P3") is a contractual arrangement to attain greater efficiency and/or access to capital. Resources, risks, and rewards are shared between the entities, and a service is delivered to the public. Roads, railways, and ports are historical examples where multiple entities, public and private, come together to build or maintain some form of infrastructure. A broadband example is the City of Lancaster in Pennsylvania, which partnered with one of its local providers, MAW Communications, to build fiber throughout town. Similar to Chattanooga and others, it originated from its water and electric utilities' needs and was financed without taxpayer investment.[7]

There are many permutations as to who provides the upfront investment and who performs the work in a public-private partnership. For example, in one arrangement, the public entity might facilitate key regulatory processes, like permitting and right-of-way access so the private entity can expediently build the necessary infrastructure. In another arrangement, the public entity may provide funding for a specific project to be carried out by multiple private entities. In the example above, the City of Lancaster secured funding, through a bond and a loan, for MAW Communications to build a fiber backbone and, later, fiber to the premises.

Another type of model, not as prevalent as the other four (yet), is the Community Wireless Network (CWN), leveraging point-to-multipoint technology to beam Wi-Fi signals from house to house, sometimes referred to as a *mesh network*. It is often built and maintained collectively by community members to provide free or affordable internet for the purpose of achieving digital inclusion. Community and individual contributions to the development of these networks may include sharing access points, donating money, donating old hardware, hosting access points, developing software for the system, and/or providing manpower and technical support to build and maintain the network. There is a variety of funding methods adopted by different CWNs. Some of these networks were built through volunteerism and donations. Others provide the service for free but charge local businesses.[8] An example is the nonprofit Tacoma Cooperative Network in Washington and NYC Mesh. Community Wireless Networks can also be used to set up service in areas ravaged by natural disasters, as a team of volunteers did in Louisiana after Hurricane Katrina. CWNs tend to spring up organically and are heavily reliant on the expertise and volunteerism of their members, making them difficult to plan for.

When discussing how the entity will interact with members or subscribers of the service, we are talking about the *business model,* as opposed to the delivery model. Most providers to the home (in all delivery models) charge a fee through a subscription business model. But some services are offered at no charge, and some are offered for free or reduced charge to low-income residents as a *sponsored service.* This was the business model that aligned most closely with Scott's vision of equity.

Going as far back as the 1990s, there are examples of communities standing up for themselves on the topic of broadband. A local "digital champion" (or a series of them) often led the way. These are communities that did not wait for the private sector "telcos" to come and rescue their unserved households. Their mission is first and foremost about serving all households in their community with a high-performance service.

But as we'll see in the next chapter, sometimes noble intentions can get sidetracked.

Chapter 9
DARK SPOTS

The problem is – building and operating broadband networks is expensive and complex. They need to be rebuilt and updated almost continually to stay ahead of the breakneck pace of innovation in this space and the constantly spiraling demand for higher and higher speeds online. And cities that come into this space are generally competing with multiple commercial wired and wireless providers – this is a business totally unlike the monopoly utility water or electric systems that municipalities have historically run.
— Katie McAuliffe,
Executive Director of Digital Liberty[1]

For years, a growing number of U.S. towns and cities have been forced into the broadband business thanks to U.S. telecom market failure. Frustrated by high prices, lack of competition, spotty coverage, and terrible customer service, some 750 U.S. towns and cities have explored some kind of community broadband option. And while the telecom industry routinely likes to insist these efforts always end in disaster, that's never actually been true.
— Karl Bode, Telecom Industry Writer and Analyst[2]

EXAMINATION OF THE PERCEIVED success or failure of a digital inclusion initiative, such as expanded broadband, requires context and perspective. Time must also be considered.

When a community decides to come together, as many have, to voice support for a broadband solution, they do so for many reasons. The phrase, "my internet sucks," often carries with it the constraints and economic limitations of an entire neighborhood or a region. There are households that need to be connected, yes, but businesses too. Where there is reliable, high-speed internet connectivity in a community, jobs and business follow, probably even more so in a post-pandemic world. There are spillover effects that are hard to quantify and always changing. A "connected community" simply has long-term economic advantages over disconnected communities. It was the same with electricity and the telephone. This is seldom debated anymore.

The community that decides to introduce a new broadband player in the market, such as a municipal ISP or a co-op, will likely utilize a subscription business model to generate revenue from customers to sustain the business. But the reason for starting up the entity is not typically *to make money*. So, judging the success or failure of these ventures solely on their balance sheets, as some tend to do, is missing the point. If the reason for a government entity in forming an ISP is solely to make money, that should probably be a red flag.

But to be clear, any fledgling ISP would need to eventually achieve financial solvency in order to sustain their business, including making loan payments. But sometimes, they just don't get there.

In the late '90s, Groton Utilities in Connecticut

wanted to be the first utility in the state to offer "tele-communications" services or a "high-speed data plan." Taxpayers voted in early December 1999 and approved a $6.9 million proposal by the utility to build a 32-mile fiber optic ring around the town. The deputy mayor of Groton at the time said that local companies Pfizer and Electric Boat had approached them and asked for a better alternative to DSL.

The Director of Utilities at the time, Andrew Chisholm, told voters they had built the idea into their strategic plan as far back as 1996. "We spent the last year studying this and discussing this in open meetings and with the council," he said. "We believe it's time for the utility to get into the telecommunications business, where we can make a return on our investment." The electric business offers only modest returns, he said, and public utilities by law can make no profit on water sales.[3]

You could argue they jumped into it to make money.

I found very little mention in the newspaper reports at the time as to the intended benefits to households, nothing about equity, and very little about any urgent need. Comcast, AT&T, and Dish were offering internet service in the area with whom the new service would have to compete. Several residents voiced their concern to the local paper following the vote about a lack of commitments from local businesses to use the service and why, exactly, Groton needed to be the first in the state. But the project moved forward, and quickly ballooned in cost. The subsidiary became known as Thames Valley Communications (TVC), and began offering cable and internet service in 2006. In the following years, the service expanded to more households in adjacent towns, raising the total cost of the effort to about $34 million.

TVC showed their operational competence in building out the network and was able to grow subscribership above 5,000 households, but this was still not enough to make loan payments and run the business. In 2012, the local paper, *The Day* reported, "Now, the city is $27.5 million in debt as a result of borrowing $34.5 million for capital investment throughout the years. Thames Valley (TVC) has lost an average of more than $2 million each year, and operating expenses continue to exceed revenues. The losses led to a downgrade in the city's bond rating earlier this year."[4] That was the last straw, and the city unloaded the operation by selling it to an investor for $550,000, leaving Groton Utilities on the hook for paying down the remaining $27 million debt.

A similar story played out in Burlington, Vermont, more recently where a municipal service, branded "Burlington Telecom," was initially approved by voters, stood up in 2006, and eventually grew to over 7,000 subscribers. But in addition to mounting debt and missed loan payments, Burlington Telecom would also suffer from financial mismanagement, with millions going unaccounted for. Burlington Telecom would ultimately be sold by the city council to a private investor in 2019 at a loss of millions in taxpayer dollars.[5]

A public-private partnership model in Monticello, Minnesota, FiberNet, was plagued by the competitive influences of the incumbent ISPs from its start (lawsuits, predatory pricing). Eventually, the private partner, Hiawatha Broadband Communications (HBC), surprisingly pulled out of the partnership prior to the end of its agreement in 2012.[6] The city soon defaulted on its bond payments and had to settle with bondholders—sounds bad—but FiberNet is still in business to this day.

Another electric utility that decided in the late '90s to upgrade its network infrastructure, and subsequently offer a service to residents, was Bristol Virginia Utilities. The offering, OptiNet, was known as a high-performance, fiber optic internet and TV package that benefitted thousands in the Bristol, Virginia, area. BVU became an independent public authority in 2010, but state and local laws barring municipal ISPs limited OptiNet's potential growth. In summer 2015, several BVU officials were indicted and found guilty of a number of federal charges including falsifying invoices, taking kickbacks, and misusing funds.[7] OptiNet's fate was sealed, and it was sold off in 2018 for only $50 million of its total $130 million price tag.

Are financial mismanagement and corruption solely the province of municipal broadband projects? Of course not. Their existence does not, in itself, make the case against taking action for an underserved community. If anything, they provide valuable lessons learned for community leaders facing the digital divide in 2021: *do it for the right reasons*. Do it to solve a specific problem. Be realistic about the viability and capital costs of starting a new service. Ensure transparency and oversight.

Christopher Mitchell and the team at ILSR reported in May 2020, "There is no evidence that municipal broadband projects have higher levels of corruption than other public or private ventures. These are problems we can all agree should be rooted out."[8]

UTOPIA in Utah, discussed in the previous chapter, was initially hailed by many as a failure, yet stands as a bright spot today. Because it is an open access network, the initial construction aimed for a huge footprint of rural Utah communities in order to attract ISPs to the market. Because of the vast expenditures required to achieve this, and an inability to meet its timelines and projected take rates, the federal government balked in reimbursing funds, and construction ceased for a period in 2006 and 2007. UTOPIA's top executives were forced to resign, and a flood of articles and studies about the waste of taxpayer dollars on municipal networks ensued.

Disingenuous as it may be to judge a venture such as this on short-term profitability, UTOPIA arguably had a big perception problem to deal with at the time. So, it hired Todd Marriott, of the hotel chain family, as its chief executive director. UTOPIA was soon able to secure a new loan of $185 million in bonds secured by its member towns, which it used to pay off old loans and continue with the construction of the network.[9] Today, it is held up as a model and a success, but it wasn't always, which just goes to show that case studies in community solutions often comprise more than just a snapshot in time. In 2020, UTOPIA was enrolling 1,000 new subscribers per month and fielding constant requests from neighboring towns to be added to the network.

"Municipal networks have gone bad," says Mitchell on the *Broadband Bits* podcast. "And I've tried to become an expert in all the ways in which they have. And it's certainly a distinct minority; there's just not many of them. But there's not one that's threatened the finances of a city. They cost less than a bridge in most places ... maybe that's not a good argument, but it's helpful context."

And the upside to many of the stories above is that the "failed" service in most cases remained available to residents — just now as a private ISP. That the "failed" entity typically remains in business as a competitor to the big ISPs in the area, like Comcast and Charter, is often a welcome and hopeful signal amid an otherwise monopoly market.

I happen to live in an adjacent town to Groton, Connecticut, into which TVC expanded. TVC is the only high-speed alternative to Comcast's internet service available in my neighborhood, and I take some comfort in that. TVC currently advertises $60 for the same level of high-speed service for which I pay about $100 to Comcast. Unfortunately, on a number of separate occasions when I called to inquire about signing up for TVC's service, the sales line just rang and rang, with no answer.

Chapter 10
EXPLORING OPTIONS

As we've seen during the Covid-19 crisis, access to broadband and technology platforms has been critical to small-business survival during this period. Without broadband, it was very hard to pivot and move to new operating models.
— Karen Kerrigan, president and CEO of the Small Business and Entrepreneurship Council[1]

The options in front of [communities], looking at the affordability barrier, were to pay for existing service — cellular through hotspot, or wireline — or build something. And I think the folks who went with the build-it solution are the ones thinking, 'This problem isn't going away after the pandemic.'
— Angela Siefer, Executive Director of the National Digital Inclusion Alliance[2]

IN ECTOR COUNTY INDEPENDENT School District, school reopened cautiously, and in phases, in the fall of 2020. The students without home internet access, those needing special education services, and other at-risk groups were the first to attend in-person. Most students were able to return early on in the fall if they chose to.

Waves of COVID cases would of course impact the opening and closures of schools throughout the fall, as they did across the country. There were still many families that chose remote learning, despite the buildings eventually being open in Texas. (By January of 2021, 35% of parents in Ector County were still choosing to keep their kids home.)

In the spring of 2020, many communities and advocacy groups had taken great strides to negotiate with ISPs individually to suspend account closures or lower rates as the pandemic shut down the country. And the telecommunications industry responded with low-cost plans and pledges not to disconnect families who couldn't pay. These were essential, but mostly temporary, stopgap measures — not community *solutions* to the broadband problem.

Relying solely on the good graces of the incumbent ISP(s) was not what Scott would call *proactive*. It is reactive. What happens after this temporary grace period? And the low-cost plans, while noble in spirit, were arguably unproductive since they capped usage and only provided the bare minimum of download speeds. Simply connecting people is not the same as ensuring they have the bandwidth for a rewarding experience online.

"It *is* an equity issue when you offer 25 Mbps to those who can't afford it, and 100 Mbps plus to those who can. Is that right?" Kellie questioned. "It's creating inequities when you say, *we're going to provide this level of service to the poor kids — but for those who can pay, they're going to get this better service.*"

While a virus raged and schools shut down, some families and teachers around the country were forced to get in their cars and drive to — *school*? There were so many stories about this at the start of the pandemic, it is hardly worth repeating here. The editorial board of the *New York Times* referred to sitting in school parking lots to get Wi-Fi access as *a national embarrassment*. These approaches can be viewed as near-term strategies to emergency needs for access, but they cannot be considered true long-term solutions for an underserved community.

Kellie and Scott knew full well they had to take the long view, in parallel with the short view.

As mentioned earlier, they were working tirelessly with the local providers, testing the Verizon mi-fi hotspots, making sure every kid had a learning device at home, working with teachers and curriculum specialists to ensure a quality of remote learning content, producing content for tv and other communications, and the list goes on. Scott didn't even want any credit for getting devices into tens of thousands of students' hands. He feels the "one-to-one" moniker, popular in education the past decade or two, has often focused on the wrong things. "I don't like to give that attention. ... It's a piece," he says, "but it's not the solution."

"The purpose of us buying those was not just so the students have a device," Lauren says, "But so they could learn anywhere, all the time."

As for the long-term view, doing nothing was an option. We called the strategy of doing nothing about broadband for the broader community, "scenario 0": waiting for the free market to work its course (amidst a global pandemic), and eventually everyone would be connected with super affordable, high-speed internet.

Sound like a good plan?

The Case for Long-Term Planning

So, at this point in the story, you might be asking: *Was a long-term strategy even Ector County schools' decision to make? Shouldn't the county collaborate with the state or a coalition of counties in the southwest U.S.?* Scott was ready and more than willing to collaborate with his fellow community leaders on something. But, what? What ideas or approaches could he bring to them? Most states have statewide broadband plans which can serve as a starting point for local planning efforts. Texas, at the time of this writing, was one of several states that did not have a statewide plan — though the Governor's Broadband Development Council recommended the creation of one, (along with an Office of Broadband reporting to the governor) in their 2020 report. The federal government has not released a broadband plan since 2010.

Pew Charitable Trusts published a report in February 2020 about the role of states in supporting the expansion of broadband access, "State broadband plans define goals and objectives, identify steps to achieve them, help guide state investments, provide a baseline against which to measure progress, and provide a framework for local planning efforts.

"Local plans, in turn, help educate community leaders and residents, putting them in a better position to carry out infrastructure projects — and apply for state grant funds when available. At both levels, planning processes ensure a systematic approach and depend on stakeholder outreach and engagement to develop robust goals and recommendations that may inform policy and program decisions. Planning processes do more than chart a path; they help educate stakeholders and build the consensus, buy-in, and relationships that are necessary to achieving goals."[3] Scott and Kellie couldn't have agreed more.

Some state broadband plans focus on the expansion of access (e.g. construction of infrastructure), while some focus on adoption efforts, like digital literacy training programs for citizens. Additionally, some are geared towards explicitly supporting planning efforts at the local community level. Pew continues, "Some state grants require or incentivize planning. Maine's ConnectME Authority, for instance, provides grants to help municipalities and local and regional nonprofit organizations define community needs, understand existing assets in the community (such as poles and wireless towers that can support broadband deployment), and evaluate options for broadband service before initiating infrastructure projects. In states that do not provide planning support, a nonprofit or foundation partner may fill this role."[4] The state of Minnesota's *Broadband Infrastructure Plan*, for example, was published in 2016 and set a goal of getting every household and business access to broadband by 2022. Based in Minnesota's Department of Employment and Economic Development reporting to the governor, the Office of Broadband Development (formed by the Minnesota legislature in 2013) also offers helpful toolkits and other community planning resources on its website, https://mn.gov/deed/programs-services/broadband/what-we-do/.

Scott has always seen great value in strategic planning — the journey maybe even more than the outcome.

Scott is a member of Governor Abbott and TEA's *Operation Connectivity Task Force,* formed in response to the pandemic. He regularly attends the task force meetings, and shared a presentation of Ector County's ongoing work with the other members. The state's Operation Connectivity included a three-phased plan of (I) purchasing devices and hotspots for students, (II) a mapping analysis of broadband coverage by TEA, and (III) a purchasing ("RFO process") effort to review offers for broadband infrastructure development. Phase I had been executed and completed in the spring of 2020. Phase II was ongoing at the time of this writing. And what phase III was, exactly, was unclear.

In October 2020, Scott reported to his board, "Many of our students in ECISD have lost over a year's worth of learning in just the last few months. That's because they're not engaged in a learning process. They're not participating in virtual learning experiences. The summer was not healthy for them, and as we started the school year for some of our students they're still not engaging effectively and so as a result we've seen some pretty dramatic academic losses that our students have experienced."

The COVID slide was anticipated.

"If you remember, we had a conversation I believe it was in May," Scott recounted, "one of our ECISD Live events spoke very specifically about the COVID slide and that was based upon predictive analytics, looking at data that indicated that our students may experience the COVID slide. And the data we saw last night (10/13/2020) was evidence that our students in ECISD have proven that claim to be true; that students, because of the pandemic and being out of school ... and then throughout the summer could experience up to a full year of loss, and that happened."

He continued. "We're working on the broadband

problem. In the short term, we're providing hot spots and then free access to our local cable providers for one year. Those opportunities are available to our parents in ECISD. We're also working on a long-range broadband project to make sure that those students that remain at home have access to high-quality broadband within their home environment."

Big Picture Options and Specific Scenarios

The long-range project Scott referred to still required a recommendation by the ConnEctor Task Force. As has been discussed throughout this book, there are many options available to a community other than just waiting around for the private sector ISPs. Each viable decision or pathway was a potential scenario to consider. *Scenarios* are a tool wielded by strategists to expand thinking and protect against groupthink, according to McKinsey.[5] "They are particularly useful in developing strategies to navigate the kinds of extreme events we have recently seen in the world economy."

"Scenarios enable the strategist to steer a course between the false certainty of a single forecast and the confused paralysis that often strike in troubled times," wrote Charles Roxburgh for McKinsey in 2009 following the financial crisis.[6] Our team decided to analyze and compare different potential solutions for Ector County in the long-range view. The hope was the exercise would reveal the best path forward for the county — but at minimum, the analysis would showcase the benefits and drawbacks of the potential scenarios for a formal task force to weigh and consider before moving forward.

A *scenario* is generally a projected sequence of

events given a set of variables or uncertainties. *Buy this tool versus that tool. Enter this product market versus that one. Go this way, not that way.* Scenario planning is the quantitative evaluation of scenarios using predefined criteria to determine the best way to go. A *scenario* for Ector County was primarily based on the idea of a strategy being undertaken to address the gaps, such as a new entity or partnership being formed to serve the community. For the long-term solution to be equitable, it would have to reach everyone, including the hardest-to-reach places. This was the primary driver. Scott and Kellie would continue to manage a portfolio of services in the near-term for families in need, (i.e. subsidized commercial ISP use, hot spots, Starlink pilot), but a reliable, community-wide solution was Scott and others' long-term vision for Ector County. One that would close the divide *and* contribute to economic growth in the region.

As we had seen in our research and bright spots, many communities around the U.S. had started up, through partnerships, a successful new service to meet the needs of the unserved and underserved in their communities. Scenario 0 would be the control, or placebo if you will, in which doing nothing was the strategy. Let the private sector and free market just work.

The widely different paths laid before Kellie, Scott and Ector County, at the highest level, included the following options:

0. Do nothing
1. Offer a sponsored service
2. Manage a portfolio of existing solutions
3. Introduce competition
4. Introduce a marketplace

5. Build a private network for school families

Scott did not believe options #0 and #5 to be viable solutions. Neither adequately addressed the issue of equity in the community. Option #2 was what Scott and Kellie were living and breathing every day, and expected to for some time, to meet the immediate the needs of their students. And it is more resource-intensive than it sounds. Especially with different ISPs in different geographies and varying coverage (gaps) for mobile hot spots. Scott started referring to the "portfolio" of solutions being coordinated for families of the district.

Most of these solutions would then be subsidized by the district (or a donor) and offered as a sponsored service to families in need, (Option #1 above). They had assumed this work early on. Scott and Kellie worked with the big cable ISPs in the area, Sparklight and Grande, to provide internet to families in those service areas who could not afford it and Verizon for mobile hot spots for students and families on the go or in areas without fixed coverage. This was the less storied and glamorized aspect of their work to close the divide. In the end, Kellie estimates they were able to get over a thousand families connected during the pandemic who otherwise wouldn't be. That is an accomplishment that deserves more airtime, but even Scott and Kellie saw it more as a stopgap versus something more sustainable; they wanted to do something that had the potential for broader and more lasting benefits to Ector County.

"I'm good with the portfolio option," Scott conceded, referring to option #2, "I don't think we're looking for a one-size-fits-all solution. Just like the education of our children, there isn't one strategy that works for all. It is a portfolio of strategies that work with children. And so, in this situation, a portfolio of providers makes perfect sense. As long as they provide a high quality of service." By *this situation*, he was referring to the ongoing pandemic with its equity issues. He would later go on to add that he hopes not to have to manage a complex portfolio in perpetuity, that someone from the private sector would one day hopefully step up. "I don't want to have to push this forever. I'd rather just have the school district at the table."

Option #4 was the boldest, most expensive, and most complex of the county's options, and is discussed in detail in Chapter 11. It was building the infrastructure around the county for a series of ISPs to lease the lines and offer services, what UTOPIA and ESVBA had done as discussed in Chapter 8.

Which brings us to option #3 from the list above. Introducing competition with a wide coverage area into the home broadband market in Ector County would theoretically lower the costs of subscriber fees across the board. It could be started up and financed with grants and loans (not taxpayer dollars), and it would begin generating revenue to pay back any loans as soon as it could be offered to residents. In many places, the city or county itself invests, builds and starts up the service, or they offer it through an organization known as an "authority" (e.g. Port Authority) — but municipal solutions like this are technically banned by Texas state law, (and 19 other states, at the time of this writing), as was discussed last chapter. An electric cooperative already operating in the county might have been the most ideal scenario, but unfortunately, there wasn't one. Still, some felt the member-owned organizational model of the "co-op" might be worth leveraging for its sustainability and demonstrated success in places like Chattanooga, Tennessee (EPB) and Minnesota (RS Fiber). The other viable delivery model was the public-private partnership, as discussed last chapter. But any of these delivery models would introduce a new entrant to the local broadband market that would compete with the established ISPs.

As we had seen in our research and bright spots, many communities had started up, through partnerships, a successful new service to meet the needs of the unserved and underserved in their communities. These models served as the basis for the "scenarios" that would be evaluated. The scenarios were defined by the type of organization that could be formed (delivery model), the business model and the network technology that would power the service. These were the proactive *do something* options that would inject competition into the local marketplace. And each would have its pros and cons.

These 4 scenarios rose to the top for Ector County to analyze and consider:

A. *Establish a cooperative Fiber-to-the-Premises (FTTP) service:* this scenario would entail leveraging existing assets (broadband infrastructure) in the region and constructing new fiber optics infrastructure to every home and business in the County; to be operated by a newly established member-owned organization.

B. *Form a public-private (shared) partnership to deploy a hybrid service:* this scenario would entail establishing a formal partnership with an existing internet service provider in the region, and develop a shared business model to coordinate and offer a new high-speed service, (a combination of fiber (FTTP) and fixed wireless offered depending on geography, i.e. a "hybrid").

C. *Form a public-private partnership (publicly funded) to deploy a hybrid service:* this scenario would entail establishing a formal partnership with an ISP in the region, providing funding and incentives (e.g. tax benefits, right of way) to expand their service to all residents.

D. *Establish a cooperative hybrid service:* this scenario would entail leveraging existing assets (broadband infrastructure) in the region and constructing new fiber optics and fixed wireless infrastructure to reach every home and business; to be operated by a newly established member-owned organization.

The major advantages of scenario A were that fiber is the fastest connection, "future-proof," and that profits would be invested back in the service to improve it or expand it over time. Unfortunately, this was also the most expensive scenario, with the longest runway.

Scenario B entailed identifying a private sector partner whose assets and operations could be leveraged to grow a new service in the region. Scenario C similarly involved the county working with a partner, but to expand their existing service and brand. This would result in less control ultimately on the part of county stakeholders and leave more responsibility in the hands of the private partner.

Scenario D (hybrid co-op) presented the opportunity to leverage the co-op model of member-owned sustainability, existing assets in the region, and local control of the service. It was less expensive than scenario A (connecting every home and business with fiber), so Scenario D scored the highest in the analysis prepared for Scott and the task force in fall 2020.

The ConnEctor Task Force had a lively discussion about the options, with some speaking very favorably of the cooperative model and its benefits. But the lack of an existing electrical co-op in the area, coupled with the perception of it being simply a rural solution, just did not align with others' feelings that a public-private partnership was the easier and faster road to travel. The Task Force also believed we needed a deeper layer of data into what was really going on in the community. A survey of families was being designed and would be launched in November, 2020. This survey would provide even further evidence than the survey performed by teachers in the spring, in that it would be distributed to every household in the school district, ask more questions, and have much more time to participate.

Regardless of the eventual survey findings, the Task Force, made up of leaders around the Ector County community, might ultimately decide to do nothing (scenario 0)—perhaps because they felt there were not yet viable options or consensus. Or perhaps they simply felt it was not the county's role.

"If the community decides to do nothing," Scott told me, "We will do something."

Chapter 11

EQUITY AND GROWTH

*The future economic success of Texas communities, and
the state in general, will likely be dependent on how
Texas uses and expands access to broadband internet.*
— Governor's Broadband Development Council[1]

*Economists have not yet agreed on exactly why there
is a mutually beneficial relationship between equity
and growth. One theory is that more equal societies
make broader investments, particularly in public
education. Another is that such societies have devel-
oped policies to share gains or pains, reducing the
political polarization that can stand in the way of
economic progress. An even simpler theory is that
such societies have realized that treating people right
boosts productivity. In any case, the idea is catching
on that doing good and doing well can go together.*
— Sarah Treuhaft, Angela Glover Blackwell,
Manuel Pastor, *America's Tomorrow: Equity is
the Superior Growth Model*[2]

FOR ECTOR COUNTY, THE proactive scenarios discussed
in the previous chapter were mitigations against further failure to connect everyone. There was simply no

guarantee it would ever happen otherwise.

And scenario zero wasn't just doing nothing about access and infrastructure — it also meant doing nothing about subscriber cost and the hit on people's wallets. The pandemic might subside and life would just go on, as if there was no affordability problem to worry about. As we found in analyzing the maps, many Ector County residents had *access* to broadband, but many were making the decision not to adopt it, likely due to affordability concerns. The survey of families, discussed in the next chapter, would seek to confirm this.

All of the potential scenarios (A-D discussed in the previous chapter) would generate revenue via a subscription business model, charging customers or members a monthly fee, as ISPs do. A rate structure would be designed for business and home users. This would include some form of subsidy for low-income individuals to pay a substantially reduced rate, or nothing at all. Lower income individuals and families would qualify for this subsidy, much like with free and reduced-price student lunch programs. This principle would be embedded in the charter and operating procedures of the entity being established. This subsidy, or sponsored service, would not be temporary or expire on a certain future date — but rather, it would be perpetual and enduring. It was building a system that ensure everyone had the broadband they needed regardless of income or zip code.

Kellie boils it down. "It's really about finding that right solution for families in the home environment. And not just for students, but for any Ector County resident or business."

To some economists, equitable solutions drive higher numbers (i.e., more people are served), which drive growth, stimulate competition locally, and result in a more educated workforce. All of those drive a stronger economy.

This is an idea that is slowly catching on.

Policy Link and the University of Southern California's Program for Environmental and Regional Equity published a report in 2011 in which the authors, Angela Glover Blackwell, Manuel Pastor, and Sarah Treuhaft present evidence, with a modern take. "Traditionally, economists thought that some amount of inequality was beneficial for economic growth; the theory was that inequality created incentives that drove people to work harder and put more income in the hands of job-creating investors.

"But this theory is now being challenged — and not only by those traditionally concerned about poverty, inclusion, and fairness. For example, Federal Reserve Governor Sarah Bloom Raskin recently stated: 'This inequality is destabilizing and undermines the ability of the economy to grow sustainably and efficiently.' A growing body of research argues that inequality is harmful to economic growth and greater equality brings about more robust growth."[3]

More recently, Marycruz De Leon and Sylvia Sanchez wrote for the Federal Reserve Bank of Dallas, "The COVID-19 crisis has communities everywhere working to expand internet access for their residents. With students taking classes online and adults working from home, community leaders recognize that broadband is an economic necessity. They're seeking ways to close the digital divide, or the gap between those who have access to reliable, high-speed internet service and those who do not.

"The shape of the digital divide is different in each

community. Affordability, infrastructure, lack of devices or skills, and low awareness of the internet's benefits can all be factors."[4]

The Dallas Federal Reserve, in believing it could spur on future bright spots, designed its own *Digital Inclusion initiative* to support the local expansion of broadband access in four selected Texas communities in the coming years. Kellie, Scott, and David met with Marycruz De Leon in early 2021 to hear about the program and share Ector County's recent research.

When the coronavirus relief package passed the U.S. Senate in December 2020, Gigi Sohn put it in context, "The inclusion of a monthly emergency broadband benefit in the COVID-19 relief bill is historic. The United States Congress, with bipartisan support, has recognized that high-speed broadband internet in the home is essential for full participation in American society, its economy, its education and health care systems, and its civic life, and that government must ensure that everyone is online, especially during this pandemic."[5]

"I'm a fan of the word, 'every,' because that means you don't leave out a single individual," Scott would tell the Odessa City Council, "What was important for us as a committee was to focus on 'every.' From an equity perspective, we want every individual within our community, child, adult, senior citizen to have access to this opportunity should they choose to. We wanted to be inclusive. North, south, east, west, city, county—irrelevant—we want to include all aspects of our community."

From an education perspective, many teachers who had never used digital tools before the pandemic were suddenly forced to. The last remaining adopter-holdouts were placed in a difficult spot. Change and growth can be hard, but there are few teachers who won't endure a bit of both for the good of their students. And what many discovered was there were different ways to engage different kids. Lauren and her team were there for those teachers to ease the transition. "We started teaching teachers *how can you create that activity but not with a worksheet?* So students are still learning the same content, but now we're using digital tools to do it," Lauren explained.

"We had so many teachers reach out to us and say *I would have never thought of that. Thank you. You just made my life so much easier.* Because you're not collecting anything [physically]. You don't have to print anything."

A survey went out to all families of Ector County Independent School District in mid-November (2020). It was sent via text message. This was intended to reach those without internet in the home, as the district had cellphone contact information for almost every family. For those without cellphone contact information, more traditional efforts would be made to extend the survey to those families: phone calls on land lines. Kellie and Scott wanted to break down as many barriers to participation as possible to participating in the survey. Had a pandemic not been raging globally, getting out to the neighborhoods, speaking with students and other residents, visiting with people at the public library, and other in-person strategies would have been employed. This was unfortunately just not possible for most of 2020.

One of the biggest questions in Scott's mind: *How many still did not have internet service in the home, high-speed or otherwise?*

Chapter 12
ACCESS AND AFFORDABILITY

From medicine to education to business, broadband access is not a luxury. It is an essential tool that must be available for all Texans. That's why I am making the expansion of broadband access an emergency item this session.
— Governor Greg, Abbott[1]

The COVID-19 pandemic has amplified the challenges faced by families and workers who still do not have reliable access to the internet. This has prevented millions from accessing vital health care, remote work and economic resources. Unreliable internet and limited broadband access has also set countless children back in school because of connectivity issues while far too many schools remain closed. It's unacceptable and hurting the next generation.
— U.S. Representatives Cathy McMorris Rodgers (R-WA) and Bob Latta (R-OH)[2]

KELLIE PICKED UP THE phone and called one of the phone numbers on her list. A woman answered. Kellie could hear the woman's voice clearly but also the voice of a crying infant very near the phone's mic, clearly in the woman's arms. Kellie could also make out the voices of additional children playing in the background. This woman was busy. Kellie almost didn't want to bother her with a survey about internet access in Ector County.

As a matter of practice, when students are first enrolled in school, parents are asked to provide many different pieces of information and points of contact: cellphone, email, home phone. In the age of the digital divide, of course not everyone fills all of these fields out, but ECISD had data on at least one contact point for each parent. This is part of the standard record keeping process. Most families and guardians had supplied their email addresses and cell phone numbers, but a few remained without the contact information. Actually, a few hundred. (OK, 956.)

Kellie stated the reason for her call to the woman with the crying infant. She informed her she was conducting a survey of ECISD families as to their internet needs which would be used to inform a plan for the county. This household was one that had not supplied an email address in their contact information, and so Kellie offered to give her the questions verbally and take down her answers. "Sure, I'd really like to help the district," the mother seemed relieved and grateful to not have to fill anything out, her children squealing in the background.

Kellie walked her through the questions. *Did they have internet in the home? If not, what is the reason? If so, are you satisfied with your service? How many internet-connected devices are in the home?* When she came to the question about testing her speed by opening a browser and going to speedtest.net, Kellie hesitated. She could hear the children in the background. Kellie knew she didn't even have a free hand, what with her phone in one and her crying infant in the other. Kellie decided what she had gathered already would be just fine. She thanked the woman profusely for her time and thoughts, hung up, and exhaled.

Then she moved on to the next phone number on her list.

Kellie wasn't the only one making calls. She had recruited a crew of 19 volunteers who were concurrently busy making phone calls and capturing survey responses manually in the waning days of 2020. They had divvied up the list to about 50 households per volunteer. It was no easy task. Some phones just rang and rang with no answer. When this happened, they would try back at a different time of day.

"I'm just worried about those folks with no access," Kellie told me one morning in early December, her voice trailing off. Their perspective and experiences had to be captured in the survey results. Scott and Kellie decided to leave the survey open through the holidays to give the maximum opportunity for households to respond. And to give Kellie's team more time to reach those less responsive. People had stuff going on. It was a difficult time.

We finally reviewed the survey results after the New Year.

The survey was ultimately able to capture 5,357 responses, which represented about 30% of families at ECISD and 10% of all households in the county. Everyone had hoped for higher numbers, but the percentages of respondents along demographic lines was very close to the district averages. Forty-eight percent (48%) of respondents were economically disadvantaged, while 56% of the entire district community was designated as such. The survey strove for representation from those that might be disconnected — but considering it had to be conducted predominantly via an internet connection (due to COVID), this number might have been far lower had efforts not been made by the landline-calling volunteers and ECISD's efforts to connect many families with hotspots and other services the previous spring. All other demographics of the respondents, such as race and spoken language, were within two percentage points of the district average, (e.g. 74% of respondents Hispanic — 76% of the district). All schools in the district were represented. Together, this provided a good degree of confidence that the findings would be fairly representative of the ECISD community.

The survey had reached 785 families without a subscription to internet service in the home (15% of all who responded). This number included those that had a cellphone, but no fixed service in the home. *What was their reason for not subscribing to internet service?* About two out of three of these families cited affordability as their reason. A small percentage of them said they did not need it, (2%). About 60 of the families reported there was no service available where they lived (8% of those without service), and the remaining respondents on this question indicated that what was available where they lived was simply too low-quality and essentially not worth paying for, (22%). This meant that 232 of these families (just under a third of those without service) did not believe they were in an area that offered a quality, high-speed service.

So, two-thirds of those without service cannot afford what is there, and the other third don't believe there is anything adequate available to them where they live.

So, where in the county did these families reside? We enlisted Whitney's help again to import the survey data (anonymized) into 5Maps to see what we could see. We were hoping the specific geographic location of these families would point towards an obvious solution or set of solutions. For example, if these families were concentrated in a series of rural pockets in the southeast of the county, a project or partnership could be envisioned to build the necessary network infrastructure out there to close the gap. Or it might show a concentration within the city limits of Odessa or West Odessa where there *is* service, indicating that costs there are likely too high and might need to be subsidized. And so on. (Or, it might show all of these things, with no specific pattern or location.) Any specific direction like this would help to target the county's long-term roadmap.

And, just as the teachers had reported in the spring of 2020: the problem was everywhere. Not concentrated in the rural outskirts. Not just in downtown Odessa. Not just here or there. Families were without internet service everywhere.

The heaviest concentrations were in Odessa and West Odessa (which is officially a separate town), and this correlated with the county population. In a problem-solving sense, this was fortunate in that many of these families lived in areas where cable or fiber service was offered, and they likely needed some assistance. But there were also pockets of households without service to the south towards Pleasant Farms, north of Odessa in Gardendale, and in West Odessa as the earlier survey efforts had also revealed.

The data showed that one in four families that responded to the survey did not have internet service in the home or had a low-performance service (under 25 Mbps download speed). Eighty-five percent (85%) of respondents were subscribed to some form of fixed service, and 59% of them reported that it meets their needs most or all of the time. Conversely, about two in five families felt their internet service *did not* meet their needs or only *somewhat* met their needs.

Maps also showed that of the respondents who believed there wasn't anything available to them, only a handful were incorrect and actually do reside in the coverage range of a high-speed service. Most of the rest were located at the fringes of the existing broadband providers' coverage areas.

Affordability was the biggest barrier. But there were also large numbers with service that was low-performance and large numbers whose needs were just not being met.

It was a multi-layered problem. And it would require a multi-layered approach to solving it.

Chapter 13
SEPARATION OF LAYERS

The simple fact is that the Internet is not the infinitely elastic phantasm that it is popularly imagined to be, but rather an actual physical entity that can be warped or broken. For while the network is designed to connect every user to every other on an equal footing, it has always depended on a finite number of physical connections, whether wired or spectral, and switches, operated by a finite number of firms upon whose good behavior the whole thing depends.
— Tim Wu, *The Master Switch*

The pace of deployment and technological progress in broadband, or high-speed, services remains seriously inadequate, a problem that results from the monopolistic structure, entrenched management, and political power of incumbent local exchange carriers (ILECs). ... It is worsened by major deficiencies in the policy and regulatory systems covering these industries. Failure to improve broadband performance could reduce U.S. productivity growth by 1% per year or more, as well as weaken public safety, military preparedness, and energy security.
— Charles H. Ferguson for the Brookings Institution in 2002[1]

Thomas Jefferson believed strongly that a concentration of power at various levels leads to despotism and tyranny. These ideas are firmly entrenched in the U.S. Constitution in the spirit of keeping certain interests apart: the separation of individual rights from government purview; the separation of the legislative, judicial, and executive branches of government; the separation of church and state. To say the least, conflicts of interest arise without such principles in place.

Senator Carter Glass and Congressman Henry Steagall worked together in 1932 to propose a new law that divided investment from commercial banking. At the height of the Depression, they presented evidence of an inherent conflict of interest in banks performing both activities and how it was ultimately harmful to consumers. The legislation was widely debated but was ultimately enacted and became the law of the land, until it was repealed in 1999. Eight years later, the U.S. entered the Great Recession.

"Big tech" monopolies get a lot of the airtime lately, (e.g. Facebook, Amazon), but *big telco* monopolies are arguably as much or more of an influence on our daily lives. How would it impact you if you woke up tomorrow and your home's Wi-Fi was out, indefinitely? I surmise that it would impact your daily schedule of activities and productivity more than would Facebook being down for a day. (Though, of course, maybe not if your business runs on Facebook Marketplace.) Home internet providers, ISPs, essentially now serve as gatekeepers to remote learning (our education), employment opportunities (our job), and visits with our doctor (our health), among many other functions. Without it, it's hard to participate.

In the communications and information industry, centralization of power not only harms the consumer, but can essentially determine who gets heard and who does not, as Tim Wu argues. At the height of its power in the twentieth century, AT&T had control of the "long lines" (infrastructure), the service (paying customers), and the hardware (telephones, jacks). In exclusively owning the various layers of production (infrastructure, hardware, support), AT&T had built a stone wall of vertical integration. This type of tight-knit control (and lack of interconnection) is extremely effective at keeping would-be competitors at bay. And these are the conditions needed if monopoly is your game.

The process of using the internet today dictates that you have four layers of tools and services: (1) the infrastructure of wires and cables connected to the internet and your home or office; (2) the internet service (i.e. the ISP you pay); (3) a device (e.g., a laptop); and (4) software. This is the vertical market stack of using a computer to perform key tasks in today's world. You also need some digital skills, resources and literacy to pull it all together. In most cases, your cable company owns the coaxial wires strung or buried all around your town, and they of course operate the service layer on which you pay your bill, call for customer support, and complain about your download speeds.

The Community Broadband Networks' webpage on *Open Access* describes, "A key problem in improving Internet access has been ensuring residents and local businesses have high quality services. One means of ensuring high quality is via competition — if people can switch away from their Internet Service Provider, the ISP has an incentive to provide better services.

However, the high cost of building networks is a barrier for new ISPs to enter the market — limiting the number of options for communities."[2]

By owning the physical wires, the cable companies are effectively able to prevent new entrants from challenging them. *Who is going to wire a town with another set of coaxial cable?* It's called "overbuilding," and as you can imagine, the entry costs are exorbitant. It just doesn't happen often in the broadband market. For one reason, the competing cable company might want to buy the incumbent one day.[3] For another, the federal government will never direct grant funding to a project where there is already infrastructure in place. Some refer to the condition as a "natural monopoly." And, as for "competitors" in a wired community, there is typically only alternative types of service with much slower speeds, like DSL or satellite, available to subscribers.

In some industries and circumstances, vertical integration is a good thing; a strategy to achieve more efficient business operations and tightly manage supply chains. But it can also easily result in stagnation or discrimination (or both) and can repress innovation and competition. When this happens in the communications and information industries, certain voices can be elevated over others. Tim Wu writes in *The Master Switch* these, "information industries, enterprises that traffic in forms of individual expression, can never be properly understood as 'normal' industries, ones dealing in virtually any other sort of commodity.

"Today, the information industries are collectively embedded in our existence in a way that is unprecedented in industrial history, involving every dimension of our national and personal lives — economic, yes, but also expressive and cultural, social and political. They are not just effectively integral to every transaction; they also decide who among us gets heard or seen and when, whether it be the aspiring inventor, artist, or candidate.

"And that creates a challenge for an American system used to a clean split between the treatment of political and economic power, a strict control of the former and only moderate regulation of the latter."

And so, it becomes time to break the internet.

Or, perhaps more accurately — time to crash the system that decides who has access and who does not.

One of the lessons learned of the AT&T monopoly was the government's favoritism towards one particular technology. This favoritism notoriously enabled AT&T to gain distinct advantages that stifled their competitors and increased their stranglehold. Thus was born the principle of "technological neutrality," the belief that the government should not craft policy that would overly favor one technology over another. This could lead to undue competitive advantages that could lead to monopoly, in theory. This principle of technological neutrality sounded like a good idea — but the idea got hijacked. Now, any time a broadband grant program has the audacity to impose high-speed requirements, a provider of a network technology with a low ceiling (e.g., DSL) will cry "technological neutrality!" The idea goes that with taxpayer funds we should be building high-performance networks that last, and only fiber optics can deliver the highest levels of service (and best ROI). So, if a federal grant program, run by the USDA, for example, were to say they are only supporting the construction of a high-performance network that delivers 1 Gbps symmetric service, this would essentially preclude all providers of internet service other than fiber optics. It "ended up as a crutch to justify subsidizing inadequate technologies," according to Christopher Ali[4], and Doug Dawson, telecommunications consultant, writes, "Technology neutrality is a code word for allowing slower technologies to be funded from grants."[5] So, the government's neutrality alone will not solve the problem.

Wu proposes a *Separations Principle* for the information economy, proposing that the different functions or layers be kept separate from one another. That those who create information do not own the network infrastructure on which it is shared. That those who own the network infrastructure do not control the "tools or venues of access." And that the federal government keep its distance and not favor any technology or other major function of the information industry. With no one controlling the full vertical stack, competition would be ensured and innovation could thrive. We saw this in practice in AT&T's 1984 settlement which separated the long-distance service, hardware and local telephone businesses into new companies.

"Like the separation of church and state, the Separations Principle means to preempt politics; it is a refusal to take sides between institutions, even naturally, bound to come into conflict, a refusal born of society's interest in preserving both."[6] Critics say it is unclear exactly how Wu's principle would ever be enforced, mandating divestiture of vertically integrated global firms and preventing vertical mergers.[7] But Wu says he offers it more as a "constitutional" principle than a "regulatory" one.[8]

In the home broadband internet services space, the ideal separation might happen between the physical infrastructure (e.g. the lines, pipes and tubes) and the service (e.g. sign-up, billing, support). This might mean one entity builds and maintains the physical infrastructure, and others can then lease the infrastructure to provide a service. This is the idea of the "open access network" (discussed in Chapter 8), illustrated earlier by the Eastern Shore of Virginia Broadband Authority (ES-VBA) and UTOPIA in Utah. The Benton Institute for Broadband and Society framed the concept as "Public Infrastructure/Private Service" in their October 2020 report on the shared-risk partnership model.

In many areas, a locality like a county government is well-positioned to build and maintain infrastructure, and to secure loans and bonds at municipal lending rates. If you need to lay fiber optic cable in the ground all around town, the county or local government plays a role, regardless. The Benton Institute's report explains, "The model also leverages localities' expertise at building and maintaining physical infrastructure in the public rights-of-way — tapping into their experience with a range of infrastructure assets from water/sewer/wastewater to roads and bridges to electricity.

"On the private-sector side, the collaborating ISPs benefit by accessing new markets, fast, without the costs and effort associated with deploying infrastructure first. ISPs can focus on their core strengths of delivering services to the public rather than the need to finance and build infrastructure. Without the need for high up-front capital outlays, private ISPs can also scale their operations to more customers in more communities."[9]

This is the ultimate public-private partnership.

The most widely documented case study other than UTOPIA comes from Ammon, Idaho. More than 100 studies and articles have been written about the smallish town in eastern Idaho, not far from Yellowstone National Park. A search of YouTube for "Ammon's Model" will bring you to a 19-minute video (produced by ILSR and Next Century Cities) in which the City of Ammon's Technology Director, Bruce Patterson, takes viewers through the "paradigm changing" approach, initially through the use case of public safety but then into the broader implications of the model. Following a planning phase, in 2014, the city essentially built the foundation for a marketplace where providers, including in other service lines like VOIP and wireless/mobile, could lease the fiber optic infrastructure and offer their service. They coined it the City of Ammon *Open Access Fiber Optic Utility*. The current mayor of Ammon has made it his policy goal to build out the infrastructure to all remaining households in town by end of his term.

The Ammon model makes it even easier for ISPs to enter the marketplace and removes a historical requirement/barrier: the significant upfront investment in hardware and resources of the ISP. Using the technical approaches of virtualization and software-defined networking, Ammon built a different kind of network. This is different from even other open access networks like UTOPIA and ESVBA that still require some investment and hardware hookups by the ISP once they agree to the lease (i.e., "manual open access"). The City of Ammon ensures the ISPs in their marketplace are qualified, and, at the time of this writing, was offering a choice of three different ISPs to households. It is among the *cheapest* super-fast broadband in the U.S., (if not the cheapest). The city maintains the fiber optic infrastructure and installs it at homes and businesses that choose to opt in. Once connected, residents can log into a portal any time, review prices, and choose (or change their service) from a variety of ISPs.

Traditional ISPs have mixed feelings about this model.

"Fundamentally, it will just be a race to the bottom," said Dane Jasper, CEO of Sonic Networks, on the *Connect This!* podcast, "and there'll be a $1 provider, and they won't answer the phone. As a service provider, I can't see the point of entering." A valid point and one that software-defined open access networks will have to address as they mature. Jasper makes the case for investment in dark fiber networks, "that is, simply glass, no electronics or optronics in the network at all — and then invite service providers in to light it — creates some really unique, positive benefits, like less complexity." It also gives the providers more space to innovate and differentiate, he highlighted.

"Dark fiber," as an approach for communities, entails the development (possibly in the past) of the necessary infrastructure for last-mile fiber optics, but not the components needed to activate it. In efforts to not dig up city streets multiple times and plan for added telecommunications capacity, historically, dark fiber was built in many places to sit and wait for the right opportunity. The city or community typically leases the dark infrastructure to an ISP that "lights" it and assumes operational responsibility.

Susan Crawford sums it up in *Fiber*: "The goal should be the construction of open-access, dark, last-mile fiber available for lease and overseen by a public authority in every part of the country to all (or almost all) homes and businesses. It has to be open access to permit retail competition wherever possible. It has to be overseen by public authorities so that it will serve the public interest in low prices and high-quality services to everyone."[10]

At the end of the day, both approaches are aimed at boosting competition in a local market. There are other examples of open access networks around the U.S., and ILSR keeps a running list of them on their "Open Access" page.[11] But in deploying a software-defined, automated open access network for its families, the City of Ammon effectively separated the infrastructure from the service, thereby introducing a new facet (even paradigm) to the ISP market.

And, in so doing, the internet services vertical was broken. (At least, in southeastern Idaho.)

Chapter 14
GOING PUBLIC UTILITY

I don't want to go back to March 2020. Because the problem is so much bigger than that. All of these gaps existed before COVID, and no one can say now that they didn't know or they were not aware. Everybody is aware of how bad it is. Everybody is aware of what needs to be done.
— U.S. Representative Jahana Hayes (D-CT)
(2016 National Teacher of the Year)[1]

It's not enough to just put up a network and give somebody a Chromebook. We have to have more restorative practices around the divides we've created and harbored in recent decades.
— Air Gallegos, Canal Alliance
Director of Education and Career[2]

WITH WHAT WE'VE COLLECTIVELY experienced through the pandemic, there emerges one essential question: *is internet service is essential to participating in today's society?*

If the answer is "yes," then all people need access to it. If all people need access to it, like water and electricity, then it cannot be left to whims of "the market" to make sure everyone gets it. It is far too important for that. Would we, as a society in 2021, have the patience to just leave it to the free market to solve a widespread *electrical divide* if it were occurring today? Probably not. (See Chapter 6) We have seen examples in several chapters of this book where market failures and digital redlining excluded people. Historically, this is usually where a utility comes in. When a community needs vital infrastructure deployed to all and maintained over time, a public utility is often the organization to do it.

In the election of 2020, Chicago posed a non-binding referendum to its voters. The question was: "Should the city of Chicago act to ensure that all the city's community areas have access to broadband internet?" Ninety percent (90%) of Chicagoans said "yes."[3] They weren't asking *do you need internet?* They were asking their residents if they felt the problem was big enough that the city should take proactive measures to address the inequities.

Colorado held a number of similar referendums. Denver, Berthoud, and Englewood asked their residents via referendum whether the town should opt out of a state law prohibiting municipalities from building their own broadband networks. (Colorado is one of *those* states, (at the time of this writing).) In Denver, 83.5% of voters said *yes*, and the other two towns also opted out of the state's broadband restrictions.[4]

This is not unprecedented, but the high numbers point to a trend.

Governor Kim Reynolds of Iowa clearly articulated her position on the matter in her annual Condition of the State address in January 2021. "As we've seen during the pandemic, high-speed internet is as vital to our communities as running water and electricity; if they don't have it, they can't grow. Every year I've been governor, I've focused on expanding broadband to every Iowa community, and we're making progress. But not enough. About a third of our counties are still broadband deserts, where high-speed internet is rarely offered. And for many Iowans, it's just not affordable. Iowa also has the second lowest broadband speeds in the country.

"I'm done taking small steps and hoping for big change. This is the time for bold action and leadership. Let's plant a stake in the ground and declare that every part of Iowa will have affordable, high-speed broadband by 2025. We'll get there by committing $450 million over that time period, which will leverage millions more in private investment, giving Iowa the biggest buildout of high-speed internet in the country."[5]

In Texas, community leaders seem to feel much the same. "Much like every family has access to running water and electricity," Scott predicts, "broadband is a utility in five years. Our families need this."

When asked about the success of Ammon, Idaho's broadband initiative and what its key component was, Bruce Patterson told *Fast Company* in 2019, "I would say it's a broadband infrastructure as a utility. We've just found a way to make it a true public infrastructure, like a road."[6]

Susan Crawford explains in *Fiber*, "There is no single meaning of the word utility, but the concept is familiar to many people. The basic idea is that a utility is a service that (1) relies on a physical network of some kind and (2) is a basic input into both domestic and economic life.

"It is not a luxury."[7]

At the time of this writing in early 2021, a lot of hype

and anticipation is swirling around broadband. The Texas Legislature is in session and considering a large investment in the expansion of broadband infrastructure, including the creation of an Office of Broadband reporting to the Governor charged with the development of a statewide plan.[8] The federal coronavirus relief packages signed in December 2020 and March 2021 will soon be allocating billions of dollars in broadband infrastructure expansion for marginalized areas,[9] and billions are also in process of being allocated by the Rural Digital Opportunity Fund (RDOF). And lastly, President Biden and Congress are on the verge of passing a $1 trillion national infrastructure plan which includes "far-reaching investments" in broadband.

And Governor Abbott certainly isn't the only governor with his eyes on broadband in 2021. "To date, at least 33 Governors have highlighted broadband infrastructure, and the technologies required for remote learning and telemedicine, as critical to closing equity gaps and for responding to both the coronavirus related pandemic and the associated economic crisis," reported Jake Varn for the National Governor's Association in February 2021. In nearby New Mexico, Governor Michelle Lujan Griffin declared, "The pandemic has reminded us that New Mexico cannot wait any longer to invest in reliable high-speed internet for all in our state. I call on the Legislature to commit at least half of their capital outlay allocations to new broadband investments, some $200 million. This is the most urgently needed infrastructure investment we can make as a state. And we must make it. Together we must put in place this essential building block and avow our unequivocal faith in New Mexico's economic future."[10]

As we moved on from 2020, and 2021 took off like

a shot, Scott couldn't help but feel a sustained urgency.

Having learned through the course of the discovery the extent of the problem and the multiple ways it manifests in Ector County, he was both overwhelmed at the scale and yet relieved to finally have some transparency into the depth of the problem. There was the support of voters, politicians and public figures for broadband initiatives everywhere he looked. *We need the capacity to respond when the time is just right*, Scott thought.

The problem needed to be tackled in phases and from multiple angles: region, county, neighborhood, and individual. A single scenario or project would not get it done. And managing the portfolio of local services to offer sponsored services to families was still somewhat reactive. At the county level, a dedicated effort would need to be undertaken to continue to coordinate with local and federal leaders, other counties, Texas's forthcoming Broadband Development Office, and other partners. This would ensure the county would be ready for opportunities to partner on the inevitable efforts at expansion and adoption that would continue to come down the superhighway.

At the neighborhood level, targeted initiatives to get families connected could be planned and budgeted for. Scott and Kellie had maps confirming where the gaps were, and as we had hoped, could point the way toward efforts to be undertaken. At the individual level, digital literacy and inclusion programs could be envisioned possibly in partnership with the Ector County Public Library to help build the skills and fluency with technology for people in the community.

"In a strategy sense," Scott reflected one day, "approaching this from the broader mindset of digital inclusion would be wise." He knew it wasn't just about access.

The Governor's Broadband Development Council shares in their 2020 report the role public libraries can play, explaining, "No single technology can effectively deploy broadband across the vast geography and diverse communities of Texas. However, libraries across the state could serve as anchors for this holistic approach by training and educating their communities in digital literacy. They might be able to set up programs to lend equipment, such as Educational Broadband Service receivers or even tablets and other end-user devices. Libraries could also serve as partnering institutions for connectivity to local government, businesses, and the community at-large in reaching the "last mile" of service access and adoption. Leveraging statewide coordination of libraries and other educational entities would help improve digital literacy across the state."[11]

Shauna Edson, Digital Inclusion Coordinator at the Salt Lake City Public Library, describes on the *Broadband Bits* podcast, "for me, 'digital equity' is everyone having easy access to use technology to *communicate, learn, work, and play*. [italics added] So, all individuals have the information technology capacity needed for whole participation in our society, civic engagement, economy, and access to essential services."[12]

She goes on to explain how various age ranges and demographics face fears and barriers to getting online (perceived and real). Those in the elder generations might be worried about accidentally wiping their hard drive clean with a single keystroke, (because they grew up in a time where that was possible) — even non-elders might face these types of fears. Some may have been victims of scams or spam. Some people may not even know *why* you would want to connect in the first place. Immigrants might feel reluctant to provide their personal information in the onboarding and sign-up process for an online service. People who can't read or don't speak English likely aren't equipped to navigate the sign-up process.

It's not enough to just put up a network. Just as it's not enough to simply put a laptop in a kid's hands.

A foundational element to addressing these barriers and building trust in people who are disconnected often means having access to an actual person with whom they can speak and who can answer their questions. It also means having someone who can coordinate various ongoing efforts in a community with a laser focus on the gaps. Most states in the U.S. have some form of governmental office or role dedicated to expanding broadband access. This role is typically focused on collaborating, planning, mapping, and funding. Another incarnation of the role is at the local level. Small city technology managers and librarians often take on the role themselves. The Salt Lake City Library has three staff members they call *Digital Navigators* who help patrons get online and answer their questions about using web-based applications.

As mentioned towards the end of Chapter 1, Scott and Kellie needed a small team to help navigate the ocean of stakeholder agendas, policy, and data. And now, they also needed help to continue the work, taking more data-driven action for specific families and neighborhoods. The needs of families were not likely to go away soon. And the solutions were not straightforward or static. For the benefit of the county and the region, in anticipation of all that was to come and all that was to change, a dedicated office or organization could be formed to build capacity to manage and coordinate future efforts for the region.

"I think everybody has to keep an eye on broadband. The idea is that it becomes a utility. That's the ending of the story: that it becomes just like water and electricity. It's going to be *that* important. Cable television will go by the wayside," Kellie predicts.

In working at the region, county, neighborhood, and individual levels, Kellie envisioned that this new office could tackle the problem from the various angles at which it presents itself but also with the holistic aim of connecting everyone. The office could be funded by, and report directly to, a board comprised of local leaders and citizens, perhaps initially the ConnEctor Task Force, avoiding telco corporate influence by design. Kellie began thinking about things like a mission statement, whether it should be an authority or non-profit, and what the job of a director might look like.

Kellie and Scott prepared to bring the idea to the ConnEctor Task Force.

The ConnEctor Task Force came together in March 2021 to review the survey results, hear from guest speaker, Christopher Ali, and discuss the recommendation of creating a non-profit office to coordinate broadband efforts for the county and region. The Starlink pilot had just launched in Pleasant Farms, but there no results to report yet. Dr. Ali, having just testified before the Senate, gave an overview of the current national landscape, citing upcoming and ongoing federal legislation and "the new homework gap."

After a briefing by David on how a non-profit

broadband office could support the local community, the Task Force members shared their overwhelming support. Nodding their heads approvingly, *"Great
idea,"* voiced more than one. "I believe it is vital to have
a person solely dedicated every day to addressing the
challenges of broadband," shared Lorraine Perryman,
former mayor of Odessa, "Without the creation of an
office with a leader that is laser-focused on the issue,
momentum can be lost and success delayed." The task
force members saw the overall vision of the non-profit
organization as an opportunity to keep the momentum
going, seize on the urgency, and ultimately close the
digital divide, laying the foundation for the community's future prosperity.

"Having a digital champion that will work on this
issue is so important," said Christopher.

In making their decision, the ConnEctor Task Force,
was choosing to do something strategic. They weren't
picking a solution and crossing their fingers. The leaders weren't putting their eggs all in one basket. They
were forming a central point of coordination for their
community to sustain the growth towards connectivity
and digital literacy for years to come. They had shown
that a group of community leaders, diverse and varied in
their roles, could come together and agree on a logical
and pragmatic course of action for their community.

"That's so powerful," Kellie told me, following the
Task Force's meeting.

The extent and depth of the broadband problem are

hard to contain to a single article or blog post. I know —
I've tried. So I hope this book has been a helpful source
of information for you to dig deeper. There is often a tendency to conflate the *broadband problem* with a host of
other challenges marginalized communities are contin-
uously navigating. But in most communities, there isn't
just a single problem going on. And so, there isn't just a
single solution lurking out there, waiting to be discovered by digital anthropologists. The internet problem in
our country must be *broken* apart into its component
pieces, so they can be addressed individually. *Segment-
ed*, in the parlance of target marketing. There are groups
of people that live in areas without service. There are
groups of people that can't afford the service they have
access to. There are some who don't want it or don't
want to engage with it. And none of these circumstances
is static. The percentages and statistics don't even really
matter in the end if you believe *everyone* that wants it
should be able to get connected. This is the promise of
a public utility. That it's just there — regardless of the
"booms" or "busts" being experienced by a community
at any given point in time.

"That connection is a basic utility. Like your water.
Like electricity," Lauren explains, "it just hurts our kids
when they're not given the access in the same way as
another kid across town, when they have literally nothing to do with that. And when you look at the future of
our community — not to get too deep — that inequality
influences that."

I used to think that the path to community connectivity was linear and easy to plot. That you just needed to find those disconnected households and find or
build a solution for them. And, actually, you can do

that. And should. But this work has opened my eyes to the multitude of barriers faced by marginalized groups even when there is *access*. This "access" must also be made *accessible*. I know Scott has never really thought it would ever be that easy to completely close the divide. It would take a prolonged, sustainable effort. But this new non-profit organization won't simply be trying to get every household in the Permian Basin connected to the internet. It will be working to ensure the community's students and residents have what they need to communicate, learn, work, and play.

This is digital inclusion —working towards the dream of digital equity.

On April 15, 2021, the Federal Reserve Bank of Dallas notified Scott that the ConnEctor Task Force had been selected to join the first cohort of their Digital Inclusion initiative. The program will offer their communities technical assistance in expanding access and adoption of home broadband over a three-year period. Specifically, the effort would fund a more technical review of Ector County's existing assets, the further deployment and testing of solutions, and the development of a business plan. Led by Kellie, Scott, and the other task force members, the foundation for digital equity in Ector County, Texas, had been forged. The work ahead was still a bit daunting, but Scott and Kellie are fearless. They had opened the doors of their schools and a window of opportunity for the community.

When asked in the fall of 2020 about his approach to the reopening of schools, Scott didn't have to think long: "Anything that we could do to positively keep our kids engaged in the learning process, we're going to do."[13]

EPILOGUE

THIS BOOK WAS WRITTEN primarily in 2020 and very early 2021 at the height of the pandemic's march across the globe, but this chapter was written in September, 2021 to provide an update on the Starlink pilot and the ConnEctor Task Force's continued work. Businesses and schools are re-opening around the world, but the pandemic has certainly left its mark — and Scott and Kellie have not lost the urgency around digital inclusion for their county.

In the spring of 2021, ECISD's pilot of Starlink, the low-earth-orbit (LEO) internet service (in beta), had launched in Pleasant Farms, Texas, and was able to connect 43 families' homes. This was about a third of the number originally planned. But to those 43 families, it seemed to be a big deal.

As Kellie had conveyed to the ConnEctor Task Force in March, recruiting families in unserved areas to a new, free internet service is not as easy as it sounds. Not when those families have likely never had internet in their homes before. Kellie explained that her team's phone calls and offers to families in rural Ector County were met with no small amount of suspicion, confusion, indifference, and perhaps most heartbreakingly, questions of worthiness. Some households essentially responded, *why us?* It was enough to bring a glassiness to Kellie's eyes as she recounted the efforts to the task force.

But this is not why the pilot was limited in number in its initial phase.

As discussed in Chapter 7, Starlink was in beta and unproven at the time. But, this being SpaceX, there sure was a lot of hype. Whether Starlink could live up to the hype has captivated the telecommunications industry since the announcement of its inception. Therefore, the results of the pilot would be interesting to a variety of stakeholders.

Starlink's service geographies are managed in hexagon-shaped cells blanketing the world. Each cell has a radius of about 40 miles. Starlink staff explained that they only have capacity for a specific number of households per cell. This was the case at the time of beta and I imagine will always be case to some extent. But the number of households per cell will undoubtedly rise as the rollout continues and more satellites are added to the constellation. In February 2021, as the pilot was set to be kicked off, Starlink informed ECISD that the number was currently only about 45, and the initial phase of the pilot would be limited to this number with the assurance that the rest of the families would be connected at some point in the future.

Starlink shipped Dishy McFlatface and other equipment in March and reported that most households set up and activated their equipment within a few days of receiving it. There were no setup or support issues reported back to David, Kellie or her team. This caused them to wonder if the service was even being used.

Starlink, as an organization was so new—keeping track of subscribers (and even invoicing) was clearly new to them. For obvious privacy reasons, they couldn't tell us much about usage, other than the status that the dish and router were activated. At the time, other Starlink beta users around the world were posting to Reddit and Twitter their experiences with the service. Initially, most were about the unpacking experience, their impressions of Dishy McFlatface and the setup. But posts quickly turned to performance, with a good deal of these initial beta users seemingly very pleased with the service.

But what about those not having a pleasant experience? (Perhaps they *couldn't* post to Reddit or Twitter.)

A survey was designed that would go out in summer 2021, giving the pilot households some time to get acquainted with the service. The survey would not attempt to evaluate Starlink's network performance, specifically, (which was evolving). And we did not need to know how the participants were using it. That was up to them. Scott's primary interest was what his families thought about the service after living with it for a time.

Engineers would say people's feelings are not a good way to measure network quality—but it is a way to measure an experience. Starlink is a service. Like many other services, it has an onboarding experience, a set-up experience, usage, and potentially multiple customer support experiences. So, most questions in the survey delved into these topics while one question did ask them to go to Ookla (speedtest.net) and run a speed test.

Personally, I was eager to hear what the families in Pleasant Farms thought about Starlink, collectively. It had been a year of anecdotes and anticipation. I was tasked with administering the survey, which meant I was also able to monitor the results as they came in. We left the survey up online for two months. I first took a peek at the results when about half the families had responded.

The results came up as a series of charts and statistics on my laptop. I blinked. I refreshed my browser to make sure it had loaded fully.

The first question asked about setting up the equipment. All respondents reported it was 'easy' (about 80%) or 'somewhat easy' to set up Dishy and the router. No one reported it as being 'a challenge' or 'very difficult.'

The second question asked if they had sought customer support from Starlink, and if so, how they felt about it. Fifty percent of respondents had and found the experience 'excellent.' Seven percent sought support and found it 'average.' And the rest did not contact Starlink customer support. No one found it below average or had a poor experience.

The survey then asked the households if they experienced any outages or significant interruptions in service. Three out of four households said 'no.' The other 25% all selected 'Yes, but not for long.' No one indicated they had experienced any significant outages, (i.e., an hour or more). (In the final results, one household indicated they experienced significant outages.)

The next question asked how they felt in general about the speeds provided by Starlink. About half said 'very fast' and other half, 'fast'—no one said 'slow' or 'very slow.'

The next question asked how happy they were with Starlink in their homes. About 2 out of 3 households said they were 'very happy with the service.' Most of the rest said they were 'happy with the service' and a small percentage reported being 'undecided.' Aside from one respondent in the final results, no one said they were 'unhappy' or 'very unhappy with the service.'

Starlink subscribers, overall, seemed pretty *happy* with their *fast* service that is *easy to set up.* "Thank you for providing internet for my children!" wrote one respondent. "Awesome service," wrote another.

A few respondents mentioned the signal dropping when they were streaming movies, even reporting that they could tell when the satellites were coming in and out of range. This is almost to be expected at this phase of deployment for Starlink. At the time of this writing, almost 1,700 Starlink satellites are working in orbit, with tens of thousands more on the way. More coverage equals more reliability for Starlink. And as more satellites are deployed, the performance of the service should go up.

As for speeds—about half of respondents (17) went to Ookla while connected to the service in July and August of 2021 and took the speed test. The test, which only requires the users to click 'Go' upon landing on the page, reports back the ping, download and upload speeds of the network on which they are connected. Ping is a measure of latency, the time it takes for the signal to travel along Starlink's network from the internet to the subscriber's home. It is measured in milliseconds, and my personal fixed connection at home is usually under 20 milliseconds, (19ms on my last test). The Starlink pilot households reported an average of 35 milliseconds. Not bad, considering that signal is being sent up into low-earth orbit and back down again, (and that the number will likely decrease over time).

The download speeds reported by the pilot households averaged 99 Mbps—and they were all over the place. One household reported a download speed of 243 Mbps while another reported 14 Mbps. The majority were in the 40–120 Mbps range. A cursory review of timestamps in the data showed that the tests taken outside of business hours reported higher speeds. But an average of nearly 100 Mbps means Starlink clearly falls into the category of broadband (most of the time), a designation that many satellite and service providers before them never attained.

If download is *consumption* and upload is *productivity*, then Starlink subscribers could be a productive bunch. The average upload speed of those households that took the test was 30 Mbps. For reference, on my fixed internet connection in my home, I usually top out around 12 Mbps. (I subscribe to a cable ISP which are notoriously limited in their upload capabilities.) The upload numbers reported by the pilot households were also much more consistent with the majority ranging 20-40 Mbps. The lowest recorded upload speed by the Starlink pilot households was 15 Mbps—still better than my fixed service's best. It is still not a symmetrical connection, of course, but it is better than what many fixed and wireless ISPs can provide in terms of upload today.

In February 2021, Elon Musk told followers on Twitter that by the end of the year Starlink download speeds would be up to about 300 Mbps and that it will drop to 20ms for latency (ping). More recently, in late summer 2021, Musk indicated that Starlink is about to exit its beta test and open the service to customers across the globe. There is ample evidence that Starlink seems to be serving their subscribers well and are pushing forward with their plans. But Starlink may always have to contend with the limited number of subscribers they can bring on in each cell. As mentioned above, this limitation is likely to ease somewhat and the number will go up. But when

Starlink is commercially available, a prolonged waiting list is what many may experience at the outset.

"To be sure, both 5G and LEOs offer important alternatives to fixed broadband," writes Christopher Ali in *Farm Fresh Broadband*, "but they are alternatives with uncertain deployment for rural America. The concern is that the rural communities may end up in a *Waiting for Godot* situation if they hold off their broadband plans in favor of these future networks."[1] *Waiting for Godot* is a 1953 play by Samuel Beckett in which the protagonists talk in circles throughout the play waiting for someone who never comes.

Karl Bode, writing for *Vice* in September 2021, echoed these sentiments, "The problem, experts say, is how many users will actually be able to get service. Limited satellite capacity means limited sign up slots, many of which will be quickly gobbled up by Elon Musk fans eager to advertise their unwavering fealty to the planet's second wealthiest human. That could leave many without access left out in the cold."[2] Mentioned earlier in the book were Musk's remarks that Starlink is not a threat to telcos and the company's own messaging of it as a solution really for those in "sparsely populated areas." The service also costs $100 a month with a $500 startup fee for the equipment. None of these paints the picture of Starlink as the "silver bullet" communities have been waiting for to connect all of their households. And Starlink never claimed to be that. Starlink will be able to connect those that are the hardest to connect – if they can afford it.

As the leader of a community, faced with diverse constituencies and geographies, perhaps the idea of a single solution should not be the goal. Monopoly is a problem enough already. Let's not perpetuate the fixed mindset that we just need to get people connected to something, and let's build a future where everyone has a choice of high-speed symmetric services to their home. A portfolio of solutions, as Scott coined it, is currently the way to make sure different strategies are deployed to serve different needs and different geographies. This will likely be the case from a community leadership standpoint for some time.

What does this mean for you?

Community leaders should continue to plan for the infrastructure necessary to connect a community with a focus on mitigating affordability issues. SpaceX and Starlink cannot do that at scale.

The Dallas Federal Reserve, partnering with Magellan Advisors, helped Scott and Kellie to craft a *Digital Inclusion Acceleration Plan* for the county. The plan included three models, variations on the scenarios described in Chapter 10, for the ConnEctor Task Force, City and County officials to consider for investment. The models were primarily about building the fiber optics infrastructure of an open access network that the City and County could lease to commercial ISPs, a topic discussed in Chapter 13. The Plan also included cost estimates for each model and began with a clear definition of the problem in Ector County.

"You might wonder why the Federal Reserve is involved with this issue," Roy Lopez of the Dallas Fed prompted the members of the Odessa City Council on October 2, 2021, "Well, this *is* economic development. This *is* job creation. And when we heard about what is happening in Ector County—what a great example of a community coming together in a collaborative effort around broadband."

The American Rescue Plan allocated billions for broadband directly to the states. Local municipalities and counties will have several years to spend these funds. The looming infrastructure bill (Infrastructure Investment and Jobs Act), passed by the U.S. Senate on August 10, 2021 and now pending a vote by the House of Representatives at the time of this writing, allocates $65 billion for broadband infrastructure and affordability efforts. The Senate legislation states, "Access to affordable, reliable, high-speed broadband is essential to full participation in modern life in the United States." [3] A striking statement for the U.S. Senate to make. You should read it again. Chapter 14 of this book began by posing the question to this answer. In many ways, it is a watershed moment for broadband in the U.S. — a *breaking* from the old ways of the internet.

Scott explained to the Odessa City Council in October 2021, "This investment opportunity (federal infrastructure dollars) provides the option for, not only our families, but for businesses to leverage the internet no matter where they are—north, south, east or west... Those communities that are ahead of the curve, that have plans in place will be the ones able to leverage these dollars." If the funding is allocated with an eye towards the federal policy failures of the past, communities that weren't connected before will get connected. Communities that were underserved may get better or cheaper service. Community leaders of un-/underserved communities must seize this moment. They should try not to be distracted by shiny objects and the notion of a single solution, but rather develop a deep understanding of the needs and experiences of the community and design solutions around that understanding.

"It requires, in many cases, innovative thinkers and innovative leaders, and it also involves collaboration. We as an organization, Ector County ISD, did not do this work on our own," Scott shared in an interview in July 2021. "We reached out to members of our community. We reached out to organizations statewide and across the country to find solutions for the problems we were faced with during the pandemic.

"We're very fortunate to find local, state and national leaders that all had solutions to the problems that were happening locally. So, I would encourage other leaders to be broad in their thinking, to be innovative and creative in their thinking. And then to reach out, first, locally and then within your state and the nation to explore solutions that are out there."[4]

Foster collaboration and the exchange of ideas. Adopt a portfolio mindset and develop a digital inclusion mindset, and you will be on your way to shuttering the digital divide in your community. You will be creating the space for all people in your community to communicate, learn, work, and play.

SHOUT OUTS OF AWESOMENESS

IN MY LIFE, THERE's lots to be thankful for. Especially the amazing team that made this book possible.

Dr. Scott Muri and Dr. Kellie Wilks put the students and families of Ector County first in everything they do. They are the kinds of individuals you want running your kids' school district. It is an honor to support them, learn from them, and help them advance their vision. I want to thank them for their input into making this book possible, and for setting an example of leadership in the face of extreme adversity. I am forever grateful for including us on the journey. When the pandemic hit and schools closed, Lauren Tavarez's immediate thoughts went to the teachers and students of ECISD and how she might be able to help them navigate and thrive in this remote learning world. She helped me understand what families in the Ector County community were experiencing, thinking about, worrying about, and feeling. She is ECISD's Director of Digital Learning, the author of the Foreword, and one of the unsung heroes. You can follow her and her team's amazing work on Twitter @ LTavarezECISD and @TechECISD.

David Irwin and Simma Reingold made this book possible, as their enthusiasm and encouragement carried the idea through, from concept to creation. I can't really thank them enough for the great friends and partners they have been to me throughout the years.

In April and May 2020, we were fortunate to spend time (remotely) with dozens of Ector County community leaders, business leaders, education leaders, technology and networking experts, private network providers, ISPs, local alliances and non-profits, and other residents. We learned so much from them, and we sincerely thank all of them for their time, insights and perspectives. A special thanks to Feliz Abalos, James Beauchamp, Wesley Burnett, Robert Chavez, Chris Cole, Renee Earls, Sandra Eoff, Dustin Fawcett, Tatum Hubbard, Gus Ortega, Brooks Landgraf, Toby Lefevers, John Nagel, Lorraine Perryman, Ray Perryman, Casey Ritchie, Ravi Shakamuri, Eddy Shelton, Brad Shook, Shawn Shreves, David Turner, Adrian Vega, Gregory Williams, Sandy Woodley, Lisa Wyman, and Jessica Zuniga.

A big thanks to Paul Donovan, who worked on major infrastructure projects around the world throughout his career and served as the Strategic Master Plan Lead for the Permian Strategic Partnership, and Jeremy Finefrock, an innovative leader at Pioneer Natural Resources Company, who have been amazing thought partners in helping us understand the landscape of broadband in west Texas, what was feasible, and what was emerging.

I also want to thank organizations like the Benton Foundation, the Institute for Local Self-Reliance, and the National Digital Inclusion Alliance for their research, insights, and dedication to sharing the knowledge so that others may apply the lessons. A huge thank you to Christopher Ali, Susan Crawford, Karl Bode, Christopher Mitchell, and Tim Wu for your writings and teachings from which I not only garnered insights and knowledge, but also the resolve to push forward with this project.

My family, Amanda and Frank, are what I am most grateful for in the world. A ginormous shout-out to them for their encouragement, their support, their patience, laughter ... for a million things I couldn't possibly list. Also, our collective thanks to Ms. Casey Miller, Frankie's second grade teacher (2020-2021), whose voice became a part of the soundtrack of our home during the pandemic and whose patience, grace, growth mindset, and recognition of each child showed us firsthand what remote learning and teaching can be. Her class's "shout-outs of awesomeness" at the end of the day gave the space for the students to experience gratitude and make it a practice. As a household, we were fortunate and grateful to have broadband reliable enough to make this possible. Not everyone does—and this book is about getting it to those who don't.

Thank you everyone!

ABOUT THE AUTHOR

TERRENCE ("TERRY") DENOYER HAS worked with government and education leaders for 20 years. He attended James Madison University in Virginia where he received his Bachelor of Business Administration, concentrated in computer information systems. He began his career in Washington, D.C. and Atlanta at KPMG, consulting for federal agencies (e.g., IRS, DOJ, CDC) on large-scale digital systems implementations. Moving to Gartner Consulting and New York City, he was given the opportunity to work with amazing and inspirational K-12 school district leaders across the country. Inspired by their passion and courage, Terry turned his attention to supporting those that are addressing the inequitable challenges in public education.

He is a co-founder of the K-12 advisory firm, Thru (thru-ed.com), and head of farm operations for a non-profit flower and vegetable garden, Hatch Fields, (on instagram @hatch.fields). Terry lives with his wife, son, and two goofy dogs in eastern Connecticut.

ENDNOTES

Author's Note

1. National Digital Inclusion Alliance, "Definitions," ndia.org, accessed October 14, 2021, https://www.digitalinclusion.org/definitions/

Preface

1. Scott Muri, "Getting Disconnected Students Access to Their Online Classrooms," *EdTech Magazine*, July 6, 2021, https://edtechmagazine.com/k12/article/2021/07/getting-disconnected-students-access-their-online-classrooms

2. U.S. GAO, "Broadband: Observations on Past and Ongoing Efforts to Expand Access and Improve Mapping Data," U.S. Government Accountability Office, June 25, 2020, https://www.gao.gov/products/GAO-20-535.

Chapter 1 | Understand the Problem

1. James Clyburn, "Allendale Broadband Pilot Project Press Conference," May 7, 2021, https://www.scetv.org/stories/2021/clyburn-officials-celebrate-innovative-allendale-broadband-pilot-project

2. Emily Donaldson, "Gov. Abbott made broadband access a priority. Will Texas students get the internet they need?" *The Dallas Morning News*, February 3, 2021, https://www.dallasnews.com/news/education/2021/02/03/texas-needs-a-broadband-office-to-address-digital-divide-for-students-and-families-advocates-say/

3. Governor's Broadband Development Council, 2020 *Texas*

Report, accessed May 17, 2021, https://gov.texas.gov/up-loads/files/press/2020_Texas_Report_-_Governors_Broad-band_Development_Council.pdf.

4. Jessica Rosenworcel and John B. King Jr., "FCC Commissioner and Former Ed. Secretary: We Need a National Policy on Internet Access," *Education Week*, August 3, 2020, https://www.edweek.org/leadership/opinion-fcc-commission-er-and-former-ed-secretary-we-need-a-national-policy-on-in-ternet-access/2020/08.

Chapter 2 | Mind the Gap

1. Common Sense Media, "The Homework Gap: Teacher Perspectives on Closing the Digital Divide," 2019, https://www.commonsensemedia.org/sites/default/files/uploads/kids_ac-tion/homework-gap-report-2019.pdf

2. Amy Klobuchar, "Klobuchar, Clyburn Introduce Comprehensive Broadband Infrastructure Legislation to Expand Access to Affordable High-Speed Internet," March 11, 2021, https://www.klobuchar.senate.gov/public/index.cfm/2021/3/klobuchar-clyburn-introduce-comprehensive-broadband-in-frastructure-legislation-to-expand-access-to-afforda-ble-high-speed-internet

3. Susan Crawford, *Fiber: The Coming Tech Revolution – and Why America Might Miss It,* (Yale University Press, 2018), 47.

4. U.S. Federal Communications Commission, "FCC Fact Sheet: Digital Opportunity Data Collection," FCC, July 11, 2019, https://docs.fcc.gov/public/attachments/DOC-358433A1.pdf.

5. U.S. Federal Communications Commission, "Acting Chairwoman Rosenworcel Establishes Broadband Data Task Force," FCC, February 17, 2021, https://docs.fcc.gov/public/attachments/DOC-370049A1.pdf.

6. Cisco, *By the Numbers: Projecting the Future of Digital Transformation (2018-2023)*, cisco.com, March 9, 2020, https://www.cisco.com/c/en/us/solutions/collateral/

executive-perspectives/annual-internet-report/white-paper-c11-741490.html.

7. Jon Brodkin, "FCC Chairman Mocks Industry Claims that Customers don't Need Faster Internet," *Ars Technica*, January 29, 2015, https://arstechnica.com/information-technology/2015/01/fcc-chairman-mocks-industry-claims-that-customers-dont-need-faster-internet/.

Chapter 3 | The Voice of the People

1. Representative Brooks Landgraf, "Landgraf Fights to Expand Broadband Access," T*exas House of Representatives*, September 17, 2020, https://house.texas.gov/news/press-releases/?id=7192

Chapter 4 | The Problem is Not Only Rural

1. Ray Perryman, "Keeping it Together! Preserving the Permian Basin Energy Sector and the Odessa Economy Through the COVID-19 and Related Oil Market Challenges," *The Perryman Group*, May, 2020, https://www.perrymangroup.com/media/uploads/report/perryman-keeping-it-together-05-15-20.pdf

2. Jessica Rosenworcel, "Broadband Discussions" podcast, FCC, November 2, 2020, https://www.fcc.gov/news-events/podcast/kathryn-de-wit-manager-broadband-research-initiative-pew-charitable-trusts

Chapter 5 | Follow the Money

1. Tom Simonite, "The Tech Antitrust Problem No One is Talking About," *Wired*, October 29, 2020, https://www.wired.com/story/tech-antitrust-problem-no-one-talking.

2. Tom Wheeler, "5 steps to get the internet to all Americans," *Benton Institute for Broadband and Society*, May 27, 2020, https://www.benton.org/headlines/5-steps-get-internet-all-americans

3. USTelecom, "Government Support Key to Bridging Digital Divide in America," July 11, 2018, https://www.ustelecom.org/government-support-key-to-bridging-digital-divide-in-rural-america/

4. NTCA, "Government Support Key to Bridging Digital Divide in Rural America," ntca.org, July 11, 2018, https://www.ntca.org/ruraliscool/newsroom/press-releases/2018/11/government-support-key-bridging-digital-divide-rural

5. Christopher Ali, "We Need a National Rural Broadband Plan," *New York Times*, February 6, 2019, https://www.nytimes.com/2019/02/06/opinion/rural-broadband-fcc.html

6. Bill Callahan, "AT&T's Digital Redlining of Dallas: New Research by Dr. Brian Whitacre," *National Digital Inclusion Alliance*, August 6, 2019, https://www.digitalinclusion.org/blog/2019/08/06/atts-digital-redlining-of-dallas-new-research-by-dr-brian-whitacre/.

7. Nolan Hicks and Natalie Musumeci, "NYC gets Verizon to expand Fios broadband to 500K more households," *The New York Post*, November 24, 2020, https://nypost.com/2020/11/24/nyc-gets-verizon-to-expand-fios-broadband-to-500k-households/

Chapter 6 | History Rhymes

1. Jennifer Onion, "A Telephone Map of the United States Shows Where You Could Call Using Ma Bell in 1910," Slate, March 16, 2015, https://slate.com/human-interest/2015/03/history-of-the-american-telephone-system-map-of-bell-coverage-in-1910.html.

2. Tim Wu, *The Master Switch: The Rise and Fall of Information Empires* (New York: Vintage, 2011), 9.

3. Ibid., 47.

4. Richard Rutter, "Independent Phone Companies Take Big Share of the Market," *The New York Times*, December 1, 1963, https://timesmachine.nytimes.com/timesmachine/1963/12/01/105228682.html?auth=login-email&pageNumber=230

5. "The Electric Cooperative Story," National Rural Electric Cooperative Association, accessed May 18, 2021, https://www.

electric.coop/our-organization/history.

6. Ibid.

7. E.G. Nadeau, *The Cooperative Solution: How the United States can Tame Recessions, Reduce Inequality, and Protect the Environment*, (Association of Cooperative Educators, 2012), 2.

8. RS Fiber, "About Us," rsfiber.coop, accessed October 14, 2021, https://www.rsfiber.coop/about-us/

9. Christopher Mitchell, et al., "Fact Checking the New Taxpayers Protection Alliance Report, *GON With the Wind*," *Institute for Local Self-Reliance*, May 13, 2020, https://muninetworks.org/sites/www.muninetworks.org/files/fact-checking-TPA-GON-with-the-wind-2020-05-13.pdf.

10. University of Wisconsin, "Research on the Economic Impact of Cooperatives," University Center for Cooperatives, accessed May 18, 2021, https://reic.uwcc.wisc.edu/telephone/.

11. Christopher Ali, *Farm Fresh Broadband*, (MIT Press), 2021, 68.

12. Cindy Cohn and Danny O'Brien, hosts, "Why Does My Internet Suck?" How to Fix the Internet (podcast), November 12, 2020, accessed May 18, 2021, https://www.eff.org/deeplinks/2020/11/podcast-episode-why-does-my-internet-suck.

13. Susan Crawford, *Fiber: The Coming Tech Revolution – and Why America Might Miss It*, (Yale University Press, 2018), 13.

Chapter 7 | 2021: A SpaceX Odyssey

1. Susan Crawford, Fiber: *The Coming Tech Revolution – and Why America Might Miss It*, (Yale University Press, 2018), 6.

2. Phil Harvey, "Musk's Starlink is 'Not Some Huge Threat to Telcos'," *Light Reading*, March 10, 2020, https://www.lightreading.com/services/musks-starlink-is-not-some-huge-threat-to-telcos/d/d-id/758092.

Chapter 8 | Bright Spots

1. Senator Markey et al., "Sen. Markey and Rep. Doyle Lead Democrats in Call to Strengthen, Expand Community Broadband," June 27, 2014, https://www.markey.senate.gov/news/press-releases/-sen-markey-and-rep-doyle-lead-democrats-in-call-to-strengthen-expand-community-broadband

2. Craig Settles, "Can Hybrid Wired/Wireless Infrastructure Stop the Broadband Hype?" *Government Technology*, January 13, 2017, https://www.govtech.com/opinion/can-hybrid-wired-wireless-infrastructure-stop-the-broadband-hype.html.

3. Jason Koebler, "The City that was Saved by the Internet," *Vice*, October 27, 2016, https://www.vice.com/en/article/ezpk77/chattanooga-gigabit-fiber-network.

4. Danville Utilities, "nDanville Project," danvilleutilities.com, https://danvilleutilities.com/nDanville/nDanville-in-the-community/nDanville-project.html

5. Lisa Gonzalez, "Court Confirms Texas Home Rule Authority to Build, Finance Community Network," *Community Networks*, October 17, 2018, https://muninetworks.org/content/court-confirms-texas-home-rule-authority-build-finance-community-network.

6. David Elliot Berman and Victor Pickard, "Should the Internet be a Public Utility? Hundreds of Cities are Saying Yes," *Fast Company*, November 18, 2019, https://www.fastcompany.com/90432191/telecoms-wield-enormous-power-over-the-internet-but-cities-are-fighting-back.

7. Hannah Trostle, "Public-Private Partnership Pursued in Pennsylvania," *Community Networks*, March 28, 2017, https://muninetworks.org/content/public-private-partnership-pursued-pennsylvania.

8. Abdelnasser Abdelaal, *Social and Economic Effects of Community Wireless Infrastructures* (Hershey, Pa.: Information Science Reference, 2013), 4.

Chapter 9 | Dark Spots

1. Katie McAuliffe, "The false promise of municipal broadband networks," *The Hill*, June 23, 2016, https://thehill.com/blogs/pundits-blog/technology/339232-the-false-promise-of-municipal-broadband-networks

2. Karl Bode, "Washington State Votes to Kill Law That Restricted Community Broadband," *TechDirt*, April 15, 2021, https://www.techdirt.com/articles/20210414/08352046611/washington-state-votes-to-kill-law-that-restricted-community-broadband.shtml

3. "High-speed Data Plan OK'd by City Voters," *The Day*, December 7, 1999, https://www.theday.com/article/19991207/DAYARC/312079959/0/Search.

4. Greg Smith, "Groton Utilities' Venture into Cable an Ambitious Idea that didn't Pan Out," *The Day*, December 2, 2012, https://www.theday.com/article/20121202/NWS01/312029942.

5. Jacob Dawson, "Vermont Supreme Court Upholds Burlington Telecom Sale," *VT Digger*, January 17, 2020, https://vtdigger.org/2020/01/17/vermont-supreme-court-upholds-burlington-telecom-sale/.

6. Christopher Mitchell, "HBC Steps Down from Managing FiberNet Monticello," *Community Networks*, May 30, 2012, https://muninetworks.org/content/hbc-steps-down-managing-fibernet-monticello.

7. Lisa Gonzalez, "Sale of OptiNet: BVU Caught Between Virginia's Rock and a Hard Place," *Community Networks*, February 12, 2016, https://muninetworks.org/content/sale-optinet-bvu-caught-between-virginias-rock-and-hard-place

8. Christopher Mitchell, et al., "Fact Checking the New Taxpayers Protection Alliance Report, *GON With the Wind*," *Institute for Local Self Reliance*, May 13, 2020, https://muninetworks.org/sites/www.muninetworks.org/files/fact-checking-TPA-GON-with-the-wind-2020-05-13.pdf.

9. Lawrence Kingsley, "The Rebirth of UTOPIA," *Broadband Properties*, October 2008, http://www.bbpmag.com/2008is-sues/oct08/BBP_Oct08_Utopia.pdf.

Chapter 10 | So, What's the Scenario?

1. Amrita Khalid, "What Biden's Plan for Universal Broadband Means for Your Business," *Inc.*, https://www.inc.com/amri-ta-khalid/biden-broadband-plan.html

2. Linda Poon, "To Bridge the Digital Divide, Cities Tap Their Own Infrastructure," *Bloomberg*, February 8, 2021, https://www.bloomberg.com/news/articles/2021-02-08/cities-try-new-ideas-to-narrow-digital-divide

3. Pew Trusts, "How States are Expanding Broadband Access," Pew, February 27, 2020, https://www.pewtrusts.org/en/research-and-analysis/reports/2020/02/how-states-are-expanding-broadband-access.

4. Ibid.

5. Charles Roxburgh, "The Use and Abuse of Scenarios," *McKinsey*, November 1, 2009, https://www.mckinsey.com/business-functions/strategy-and-corporate-finance/our-insights/the-use-and-abuse-of-scenarios#

6. Ibid.

Chapter 11 | Equity and Growth

1. Governor's Broadband Development Council, "2020 Texas Report," Office of the Governor, https://gov.texas.gov/uploads/files/press/2020_Texas_Report_-_Governors_Broadband_Development_Council.pdf

2. Angela Glover Blackwell, et al., "America's Tomorrow: Equity is the Superior Growth Model," *Policy Link*, 2011, https://www.policylink.org/sites/default/files/SUMMIT_FRAMING_WEB_20120110.PDF.

3. Ibid.

4. Marycruz De Leon and Sylvia Sanchez, "How Can You Close

the Digital Divide in Your Community? Start with a Needs Assessment," *Federal Reserve Bank of Dallas*, September 14, 2020, ttps://www.dallasfed.org/cd/communities/2020/0914.

5. Gigi Sohn, "Sohn Cheers Inclusion of "Historic" Emergency Broadband Benefit in COVID-19 Relief Bill," gigisohn.com, December 21, 2020, http://gigisohn.com/media/sohn-cheers-inclusion-of-historic-emergency-broadband-benefit-in-covid-19-relief-bill/

Chapter 12 | Access and Affordability

1. Emily Donaldson, "Gov. Abbott made broadband access a priority. Will Texas students get the internet they need?" *The Dallas Morning News*, February 3, 2021, https://www.dallasnews.com/news/education/2021/02/03/texas-needs-a-broadband-office-to-address-digital-divide-for-students-and-families-advocates-say/

2. "E&C GOP Leaders Unveil the Boosting Broadband Connectivity Agenda," Energy and Commerce Committee, February 16, 2021, https://republicans-energycommerce.house.gov/news/press-release/ec-gop-leaders-unveil-the-boosting-broadband-connectivity-agenda/.

Chapter 13 | Separation of Layers

1. Charles H. Ferguson, "The U.S. Broadband Problem," *Brookings Policy Brief Series*, July 31, 2002, https://www.brookings.edu/research/the-u-s-broadband-problem/

2. Community Networks, "Open Access," Institute for Local Self-Reliance, https://muninetworks.org/content/open-access

3. Brian Fung, "One Fascinating Reason Cable Companies Won't Willingly Compete Against Each Other," *Washington Post*, May 24, 2016, https://www.washingtonpost.com/news/the-switch/wp/2016/05/24/the-reason-cable-companies-wont-willingly-compete-against-each-other/.

4. Christopher Ali, *Farm Fresh Broadband*, (MIT Press, 2021), 73

5. Doug Dawson, "Technology Neutrality," *Pots and*

Pans, September 29, 2021, https://potsandpansbyccg.com/2021/09/29/technology-neutrality/

6. Tim Wu, *The Master Switch: The Rise and Fall of Information Empires* (New York: Vintage, 2011), 304.

7. Brent Skorup and Adam D. Thierer, "Uncreative Destruction: The Misguided War on Vertical Integration in the Information Economy," *Federal Communications Law Journal*, April, 2013, https://dx.doi.org/10.2139/ssrn.2162623.

8. *University of Chicago Law Review*, Vol. 8, Number 4, Fall 2012, https://www.google.com/books/edition/University_of_Chicago_Law_Review_Volume/olwbAgAAQBAJ?hl=en&gbpv=1 &pg=PT624&printsec=frontcover

9. Joanne Hovis, et al., "Public Infrastructure/Private Service: A Shared-risk Partnership Model for 21st Century Broadband Infrastructure," *Benton Institute for Broadband & Society*, October 2020, https://www.benton.org/sites/default/files/PPP3_final.pdf.

10. Susan Crawford, *Fiber: The Coming Tech Revolution – and Why America Might Miss It*, (Yale University Press, 2018), 205.

11. Community Networks, "Open Access," Institute for Local Self-Reliance, https://muninetworks.org/content/open-access

Chapter 14 | Going Public Utility

1. Jahana Hayes, "Cross Connection," MSNBC, January 30, 2021, https://fb.watch/5HPca56iP5/

2. ILSR, "Community Broadband Bits" podcast, Episode 427, September 17, 2020

3. Lynda Lopez, "Broadband on the Ballot," *South Side Weekly*, October 14, 2020, https://southsideweekly.com/broadband-on-the-ballot/.

4. Ryan Johnston, "Chicago, Denver Voted to Take Broadband 'Seriously' on Tuesday," *Statescoop*, November 5, 2020, https://statescoop.com/

chicago-denver-voted-to-take-broadband-seriously-on-tuesday/.

5. Governor Kim Reynolds, "2021 Condition of the State," January 12, 2021, https://governor.iowa.gov/press-release/gov-reynolds-delivers-2021-condition-of-the-state

6. Jay Woodruff, "The City with the Best Fiber-Optic Network in America Might Surprise You," *Fast Company*, October 21, 2019, https://www.fastcompany.com/90416863/the-city-with-the-best-fiber-optic-network-in-america-might-surprise-you.

7. Susan Crawford, Fiber: *The Coming Tech Revolution – and Why America Might Miss It*, (Yale University Press, 2018), 161.

8. "Nichols and Ashby to File Legislation Expanding Broadband Services," Texas House of Representatives, January 7, 2021, https://house.texas.gov/news/press-releases/?id=7238.

9. Stephaine Kanowitz, "Broadband Access Moves up Government's Priority List," GCN, January 5, 2021, https://gcn.com/articles/2021/01/05/broadband-imperative.aspx.

10. Jake Varn, "Governors Start 2021 by Expanding Access to Broadband," *National Governors Association*, February 16, 2021, https://www.nga.org/news/commentary/governors-expanding-access-broadband-2021.

11. Governor's Broadband Development Council, *2020 Texas Report*, accessed May 17, 2021, https://gov.texas.gov/uploads/files/press/2020_Texas_Report_-_Governors_Broadband_Development_Council.pdf.

12. ILSR, "Transcript: Community Broadband Bits Episode 442," Community Broadband Bits podcast, January 21, 2021, https://muninetworks.org/content/transcript-community-broadband-bits-episode-442

13. Lauren Jackson, "Odessa," The New York Times, February 26, 2021, https://www.nytimes.com/2021/02/26/podcasts/odessa-school-reopenings-texas.html

Epilogue

1. Christopher Ali, *Farm Fresh Broadband*, (MIT Press, 2021), 298.

2. Karl Bode, "Elon Musk's Starlink Won't Be the Game Changer You Think," Vice, September 17, 2021, https://www.vice.com/en/article/3aq9e8/elon-musks-starlink-wont-be-the-game-changer-you-think

3. U.S. Senate, "H.R.3684 - Infrastructure Investment and Jobs Act," congress.gov, August 10, 2021, https://www.congress.gov/bill/117th-congress/house-bill/3684/text

4. Roger Riddell, "Lessons In Leadership: How a superintendent tapped SpaceX to help close homework gap," *K-12 Dive*, July 20, 2021, https://www.k12dive.com/news/lessons-in-leadership-how-a-superintendent-tapped-spacex-to-help-close-hom/603587/

www.ingramcontent.com/pod-product-compliance
Lightning Source LLC
Chambersburg PA
CBHW071417210326
41597CB00020B/3551